Vintage Camper Trailer Rallies

STARFIRE
CALIFORNIA
EWA 606

Vintage Camper Trailer Rallies

PAUL AND CAROLINE LACITINOLA

GIBBS SMITH
TO ENRICH AND INSPIRE HUMANKIND

This book is dedicated to those that helped us complete it in a year when we were overcommitted in other aspects of the hobby. We were busy hosting and attending rallies, lecturing, and doing our own trailer restorations. We could not have done it without the contributions from photographers, writers, and trailerites who contributed some of the content. Special thanks to senior editor Bob Cooper of Gibbs Smith, who patiently pulled it all together into a book that we can all enjoy.

First Edition
22 21 20 19 18   5 4 3 2 1

Published by
Gibbs Smith
P.O. Box 667
Layton, Utah 84041

1.800.835.4993 orders
www.gibbs-smith.com

Designed by Rita Sowins / Sowins Design
Printed and bound in Hong Kong

Gibbs Smith books are printed on paper produced from sustainable PEFC-certified forest/controlled wood source. Learn more at www.pefc.org.

Library of Congress Cataloging-in-Publication Data
Names: Lacitinola, Paul, author. | Lacitinola, Caroline, author.
Title: Vintage camper trailer rallies / Paul and Caroline Lacitinola.
Description: First edition. | Layton, Utah : Gibbs Smith, [2018]
Identifiers: LCCN 2017032827 | ISBN 9781423647676 (hardcover)
Subjects: LCSH: Camping trailers--Collectors and collecting. |
  Automobiles--Societies, etc. | Automobiles--Exhibitions.
Classification: LCC TL297 .L329 2018 | DDC 629.226075--dc23
LC record available at https://lccn.loc.gov/2017032827

Photo by Hal Thoms Photography.

Contents

Acknowledgments

We would like to thank the following people and organizations for the help they provided in the creation of this book: Rich Luhr of *Airstream Life* magazine (www.airstreamlife.com); the Wally Byam Caravan Club International (WBCCI.org); photographer Dale Godfrey (www.godfreyphoto.com); photographer Hal Thoms; and Terry Bone of Tin Can Tourists. We'd also like to acknowledge the book *Airstream: America's World Traveler* by Patrick Foster, which proved an invaluable resource for us.

This Spartanette reflects the vintage feel at Palm Springs Modernism Week. Photo by Hal Thoms Photography.

DeVille

Introduction: Our Story

As a kid in the 1970s, Paul grew up on a five-acre almond orchard in Chico, California, where his family had plenty of room for forgotten treasures. One of those treasures was a dilapidated Shasta trailer in the backyard. His grandfather was a wannabe gold prospector and stayed in the trailer at his mine. When the mining endeavor ended, the trailer was retired to the yard. For reasons unknown, the sixteen-foot trailer's door was missing by the time it got to the Lacitinola's place. The old trailer was not in great repair, even though it would have only been ten to fifteen years old at the time. It served Paul and his two younger brothers as a playhouse during the 1970s. It was everything from a police station for 1-Adam-12 to a fire department for Squad 51. Back then, people had no appreciation for what today is a highly sought-after classic.

Pop (Angelo Lacitinola) standing on the running board of his 1954 International Harvester R110 pickup, ca. 1980s. Pop bought this pickup in the early 1960s and it has always been in our family. It will be our son Angelo's first car.

In the 1960s, Paul's father, Paul Sr., owned the Shasta Service Color used car lot with his father, Angelo Lacitinola. The name "Shasta" was used because of the views of Mount Shasta; it had nothing to do with Shasta trailers, although the Shasta trailer dealer was about a half mile up the road. The phone number was FI2-9759. Back then the property was four miles from the town of Chico. Today it is covered with apartments and is bordered by an elementary school and public parks. The Paul and Angelo named on the business card are Paul's father and grandfather, but it could as well be for Paul and our son, who share the same names.

In 2006, with two kids, Angelo and Grace, who were under three years old, we decided that we wanted to go camping. Our neighbors were selling their 1962 DeVille camper trailer and we couldn't resist dragging it home. We purchased our first vintage trailer not because we thought it was cool, but because it was cheap. We wanted to go camping, but we did not want to invest a lot of money in a trailer. Not knowing if we would like the RVing lifestyle, an inexpensive, older trailer seemed good enough for us. As owners of classic cars, the idea of buying something old and fixing it up made sense to us. The whole family was excited to go camping in our "new" old trailer, but we had no idea how that simple $500 purchase would change our lives in such a positive way, forever.

Prior to buying our '62 DeVille, we don't know if we had ever noticed vintage trailers, much less thought the idea of camping with strangers might be enjoyable. When we began camping as a family in our twelve-foot trailer we liked getting away with its modest amenities. We were often stopped by fellow campers as they commented on how neat the little old trailers were, and reminisced about the time they spent camping in trailers from a bygone era. We quickly realized that people had a real emotional connection with vintage trailers. As an old-car guy, Paul got it. He started to see our cheap old trailer as more of a classic and thought, "How cool would it be to put it behind an old car?" Paul decided that the classic car world would really love vintage camper trailers and wrote an article for our local car paper, *Cruisin' News*.

Shasta Service Station, Chico, California, owned by Paul's grandparents Angelo and Ruby Lacitinola, ca. 1950s. Their businesses on the north end of the Esplanade included four motel-room "cabins," an automotive shop, and a convenience market with fuel pumps. From behind the counter of the store you could walk right into Nana's kitchen. Pop had a used car lot and a junkyard of cars out back for parts. When Paul was a kid, he and his brothers and cousins played in and on the broken-down cars from the 1930s, '40s and '50s. Drawing by Paul's dad's cousin, Anthony Passarelli.

Paul Lacitinola Sr. in a Model A "roadster" crafted from a coupe.

The DeVille's interior is all original. The wood finishes on the cabinets do not match the finish on the walls. The tiki cookie jar is a reminder of Paul's childhood, as it was always on the kitchen counter in his house.

Paul has always been an old car guy. Growing up, his notebooks in school were covered with drawings of T-bucket roadsters and 1930s coupes. In high school he drove a 1964 Chevelle and a 1957 Chevy. As an adult he's almost always had a vintage car or two. His most recent acquisition was a 1936 Ford five-window coupe. Paul's father drove a '36 Ford when he was in high school. Black-and-white pictures like this one of the "Blue Charmer" most certainly made an impression on Paul. Like the trailers, many of us also have a connection to a certain year, make, or model of a car from our past.

The 1962 Deville on a camping trip with our church. Caroline's red vintage bike pairs well with any old trailer.

When Paul wrote his first article telling people about old trailers, he thought he had invented the vintage trailering hobby. He was unaware that anybody, anywhere, had even noticed these pieces of Americana. Optimistic that he'd discovered the next new craze in collecting, he was eager to share the idea with others. It didn't take long to learn that he was not the first one to the party. John and Phyllis Green read that first article in *Cruisin' News* and called us. They invited us to a rally at the Tower Park Marina campground in Lodi, California. What?! How could this be? Somebody else thought of this already! Paul and our daughter, Grace, visited the rally and met the Greens. They were camping in their 1949 Westcraft Trolley Top. The Greens and their friends, in about a dozen vintage trailers, were scattered around a section of this shady campground located in the California Delta. To this day the Westcraft Trolley Top trailer is Paul's favorite, and one that we are still looking for to add to our collection. We took pictures of all the trailers at the campout so Paul could use them with his next article. Paul and Grace spent the day learning about the hobby and all the different trailers from these hobby veterans. The Greens invitation into the group led to meeting other trailerites like Wayne and Kathy Ferguson, and Penny Cotter and Charlie Nienow. They had already restored vintage trailers and were getting together at rallies. They were just a few of the people that welcomed us into the hobby in the beginning, and have become great friends over the past decade.

Once reality hit that we hadn't created a new hobby, we were happy to rally with other fellow old souls who had a passion for the same things we did. There was no vintage camper trailers magazine to tell you where the rallies were, so networking with people in the hobby was imperative. Penny Cotter was the newly appointed regional Tin Can Tourist representative, and she was organizing a rally at a campground in Coloma, California. By now we had purchased our second trailer, a 1959 Shasta Deluxe. We got the trailer from the original owner, Joy Billingsley. Joy's father bought the trailer new and used it for decades for his hunting and fishing trips. The Shasta was eventually retired to a storage area in Joy's backyard and would likely still be there if Joy had not decided to build an addition to her home. The awning that had

We heard about a Shasta for sale in Los Angeles and made the trip from Sacramento not knowing if we would ever find another rare Shasta! Here is our 1959 Shasta Deluxe as we found it in the original owner's backyard. Angelo was little then but could still kick the tires.

sheltered the trailer for years had to come down, and Joy decided it was time to let someone else enjoy their family's old trailer that had served them so well for decades.

At the next rally in Coloma we couldn't have been prouder showing up in our original, unrestored Shasta! Bigger than the DeVille, the Shasta was a Deluxe Model 19. It had two bunks for the kids and a bathroom. Now we were living! The Billingsleys had painted the trailer brown years ago to match their truck. We eventually changed the trailer's color back to its original yellow and cream, but we left the interior in its very good, original, unrestored condition and have never disturbed the medicine cabinet that Joy's dad built way back when. It is still packed full of vintage first aid gear, just in case we have an emergency.

The Shasta's interior the first time we laid eyes on it.

The Shasta was not only in incredible condition, but also held many period treasures that came with it.

Angelo and Grace in the 1959 Shasta.

Angelo and Grace were so little they had to sit on boxes to reach the table. The 1962 DeVille in original paint sits in the background.

Caroline, Paul, Angelo, and Grace with their restored 1959 Shasta.

The first vintage trailer rally we attended had us hooked. Seeing the variety of trailer makes, models, and sizes was an eye-opener. Never had we paid attention to old trailers, much less admired them and the individuality each one, and their owners, seemed to have. A new world of collectors and restorers was opened to us. The "trailerites" welcomed us as one of their tribe, and as we have heard many others say since then, "we had found our people."

At that time there were fewer rallies than there are today. It didn't take long to hear about the rally at Pismo Beach—a rally that boasted 300 trailers, many more than other rallies. The Pismo Rally is a sellout every year, but we got on the waiting list and were able to get a site. We proudly took our 1962 DeVille, which by this time we had spent hours polishing and painting the original exterior aluminum siding to make it show worthy. We had also done some minor restoration and refinishing to the interior wood paneling and installed new flooring. We were excited to debut our many hours of effort that we had invested in our unusual vintage trailer. With over 300 miles ahead of us, we set out with the kids, bikes, and enough food for a month.

On the way to the rally we decided to stop to stretch and grab a bite to eat. While driving through a small town just off the highway, we passed three young adult men who were playfully pushing and shoving each other on the sidewalk. As we passed, one of the men fell off the sidewalk into the traffic and in between the rear of our tow vehicle and the front of our trailer. Caroline happened to be looking in the passenger-side rearview mirror and saw it happen. The man struck the front of our trailer and narrowly missed being run over with the trailer tire. Although we did not feel the impact, it was substantial enough to crush the corner of our just-polished aluminum skin and even break the plywood on the interior behind the booth seating! The young man was taken to the hospital by ambulance and we were back on our way, bruised and somewhat shaken, but still looking forward to what the weekend had in store for us. (The injured man was treated and released.)

About an hour down the road, still hungry and in disbelief of what had happened, we had another surprise. At 55 mph, the driver-side trailer wheel came off the hub! In the middle of nowhere, along a two-lane highway with no shoulder, we pulled to the right as far off the road as we possibly could. The trailer's wheel and tire had bounded across oncoming traffic and careened through a farmer's white PVC fence that marked the entryway to his farm. The plastic fencing was only a few sections on either side of the driveway, but our candy apple–red wheel and fifteen-inch tire, still traveling at highway speed, snapped the middle rung of the right-hand side of the fence like it was balsa wood! The wheel barely slowed down as it crossed an open field before coming to a stop in the cattails that lined the banks of the canal that ran under the highway just ahead. We apologized to the farmer's wife for the damage to the fence and let her know where to send the bill, before fishing our wheel out of the canal.

At one point (as Caroline claims), Paul said, "Get back in the truck, we're going home!" That is exactly what we felt like doing. Instead, we unhooked the trailer and Paul headed for the next town for parts while Caroline and the kids stayed with the DeVille. Perched on a bottle jack, the trailer swayed precariously with each big rig that whizzed by at 70 mph. Our front right corner was dented from the human impact a mere sixty minutes earlier and the left side of the trailer siding was torn and mangled from the wheel well back. When the wheel left the hub, it went up inside the wheel well and broke out the sink cabinet inside the trailer before tearing up the aluminum siding and finally snapping the farmer's fence.

Grace kept a positive attitude when we wrecked the 1962 DeVille on our way to the Pismo Rally.

In town, Paul found new lugs and nuts, and was able to repair the hub to get us back on the road. We got a hotel and spent that night regrouping and "duct-taping" our trailer back together for the big rally! We learned a very important lesson: *Always double check that your lug nuts are tight.*

Our first year at Pismo we were like kids in a candy store. We spent hours trying to see all of the incredible coaches, inside and out. All the vintage bicycles, Cushman scooters, and classic cars were overwhelming. Paul would later reflect that his first year at the Pismo Rally, skydiving, and being in a vehicle pursuit (when he was a police officer) were the biggest adrenaline rushes he had ever experienced. We never did get a bill for the fence (maybe they felt sorry for us), and we had an incredible tale to tell all who stopped to see our battered little trailer that weekend.

We started hosting rallies almost by accident. In 2011 we wanted to get a group of friends together and go camping. We called around and found out that the KOA campground at Tower Park in Lodi was having an event they called "Towerfest." It was a tiki-themed event complete with hula dancers, food, and all the amenities the park had to offer. That year there were less than two dozen of us and we had a blast. The next year when we put the word out over fifty trailers registered. Over a span of six years we worked with different park managers and even new owners when Yogi Bear's Jellystone Park Camp-Resorts purchased the park from KOA in 2016. Towerfest became "Trailerfest" after the park quit hosting that event. By our fourth year we were selling out the entire park, with over 250 trailers and all the cabins filling up months in advance and waiting lists of people who wanted to come. In 2016 the new owners of the park let us know that their future plans included more cabins and less campsites. Already busting at the seams, we had to find a different park with at least as many campsites. After much searching we ended up at 49er Village in Plymouth, California.

Grace in her Team VCT T-shirt at Trailerfest with Santa and Mrs. Claus.

Our 1948 Vagabond

This 1948 Vagabond is a trailer that we restored with help from our good friends Tim and Linda Brown. Jimmy Proctor did the incredible paintwork in the original color we found under a marker light. The restoration is very close to the original, and the decorations are all postwar and period correct, from Paul's mom's side of the family. The photos are of Paul's grandmother and grandfather, Madeline and Joe Brandt. The silk quilt (see page 20) came from a family trunk, and the fox pelt (see page 20), an element that was in vogue from the 1920s through the 1940s, was trapped in Alaska by Caroline's brother.

Vagabond trailers were built in New Hudson, Michigan, from 1931 to 1957. This one is a 1948 Model 19 (nineteen feet long). The original models were Masonite-sided trailers, but by 1937 the design included a welded steel chassis made of 1 x 1 inch square tubing.

Our Vagabond is decorated with family memorabilia from the late 1940s.

A family photo album from the early '40s on display.

This original table is attached to the wall with a hinge that allows it to swing out away from the wall or fold up against the wall providing more floor space.

The bedroom is at the rear of the trailer and has a sliding door for privacy. The silk patchwork quilt is a family piece from the '40s, and the fox was trapped in Alaska by Caroline's brother, Steve. In the 1940s, furs were the definition of elegance.

Popular Vagabond models ranged from about nineteen to twenty-nine feet in length, and featured birch interiors and aluminum exterior siding.

The original appliances are
still in good working order.

In 1957, Vagabond moved into the ten-wide
market with mobile home models that were
thirty-five, forty-one, and forty-six feet long.
Trailer manufacturers and industry insiders
were positioning their product as a symbol
of progress, wealth, leisure, and modernism.

There were many others that preceded us in finding and restoring trailers. For the past ten years Paul has continued to write an article each month for *Cruisin' News,* and we have attended several rallies every year. We went from being one of the newbies to one of the trailerites welcoming newcomers to the hobby. Around 2006 Facebook became available to everyone with a valid e-mail address. The social media platform made it possible to network with others with similar interests. We started a very simple website and a Facebook page to share all the fun we were having. The Facebook page now has nearly 600,000 followers.

Social media connected people, and people liked what they saw. Rallies were selling out, so more rallies were started by courageous first-time wagon masters. The demand for vintage trailers increased and so did the prices to acquire a trailer. This once underground hobby, known only to a select few, started to grow. For old-car guys, the transition seemed natural, but the largest segment of the hobby was women. Whether it is the nesting, glamping, or tiny house feel that is the attraction to the little canned hams, women make up more than 50 percent of the hobby. It is not uncommon for a husband and wife to enjoy the hobby with a classic car and a vintage trailer. No longer does an outing consist of sitting at a car show in a lawn chair on asphalt while eating fast food. At a rally we get to bring our beds and great food and make a weekend out of it!

This book is our response to all the people like us that want to host a vintage trailer rally. We have personally shared with many what we have learned, and decided that it would reach a wider audience if we put it into a book. We hope this book will give you an insight into what it takes to host a rally, and help you determine if you are ready and cut out for the task. We now host several rallies and events each year and have included everything we have learned to help you either host your own event or be a good attendee for the individuals who have decided to take on the role of wagon master.

Always made in the USA.

Visitors to an openhouse at a rally in Buellton, California, get to see a restored 1948 Vagabond Model 19 up close.

Eric and Erika Frye's 1963 Shasta

In 1941 the first Shasta house trailers were built for use as mobile military housing. Today Shasta trailers are some of the most sought-after models. They are easily identifiable by the wings on most models, and the 1950s and '60s models have one of the most recognizable shapes on the road. Some say it looks like a toaster on wheels more than a canned ham.

Eric and Erika Frye's 1963 Shasta 16 SCS smelled of dead animals and dogs when they bought it in the desert outside of Las Vegas. It was a complete mess, with spare tires covering holes in the floor and gun racks screwed into the exterior siding. The Fryes' daughters, Hannah and Sydney, were horrified when their parents brought the trailer home and parked it in their front yard. Undaunted by their children's lack of vision, Eric and Erika set to work restoring "Neptune." New electrical, plumbing, cabinets, siding, and exterior paint were applied to the Shasta. Erika's dream is to one day live by the ocean. Until then, she's decorated her vintage trailer to match her dream. Now Hannah and Sydney love the little trailer and enjoy camping in it with their parents. Sydney even dreams of one day owning her own vintage trailer.

All photos on pages 24–25 by Dale Godfrey.

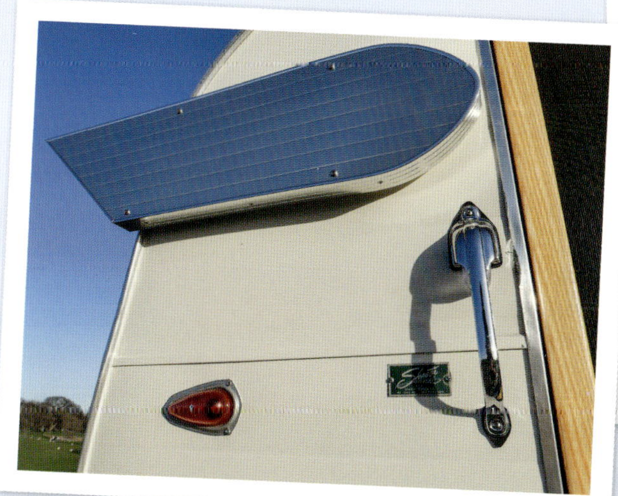

SANDY

LIFE
SPECIAL
ISSUE

5E 346
CAL 39

CHAPTER 1

The History of Rallies

A band or tribe of people living in the wilderness could be a description of prehistoric man or the definition of a camping rally. People have always gotten together and enjoyed the great outdoors. What we call a "vintage trailer rally" can vary from a handful of trailers to several hundred enthusiasts gathered together to socialize. No matter how many are in attendance we always find the tribe welcoming to the newcomer, without regard for the caliber of their camper trailer.

The 1930s Covered Wagon camping trailer shown here took its name from its horse-drawn predecessor. Another brand built in the 1940s, the Prairie Schooner, was named after the nineteenth-century wagons used by emigrants traveling to the American West, whose white canvas covers from a distance appeared to be a schooner's sail moving across the open prairie.

Facing page: Linus Tremaine purchased his 1930 Lincoln Model L Type 177 sport touring car and 1935 Gilkie Deluxe tent trailer from two different owners who had taken good care of these classics. The Lincoln was part of a fleet of cars used at the CM Ranch in Dubois, Wyoming, all of which were painted green. Following it's fleet life, it was purchased by Lincoln collector Jack Passey, who owned it for fifty years. The Gilkie was purchased in 2000 by trailer collector Bob West, who restored the trailer to close to its original condition, leaving the original paint and interior; the top fabric and the canvas have been replaced.

Covered Wagon

A 1934 Covered Wagon restored by Flyte Camp of Bend, Oregon. The exterior of the Covered Wagon is covered with leatherette siding and has a period-correct canvas top that mimics the unique construction method that was originally used. (Leatherette is an imitation leather product commonly used in the marine industry.)

Period-correct knickknacks that represent the era of the trailer give it a real feel of vintage elegance.

An unusual floor plan has the "dining room" at the rear of the trailer, and the dinette converts into a bed.

Bathrooms were not commonplace in prewar trailers. This would have been a deluxe accommodation.

A toaster that would have been used in the 1930s is right at home in this trailer.

The Flyte Camp crew restored the original wood-burning stove.

The original flooring, Coleman hot plate, and leaded glass in the galley cabinets, as well as the intricate 1930s hardware on the doors and cupboards, are all original.

The history of the modern camping rally can be traced back to the turn of the twentieth century. Prior to the popularity of cars, the closest thing to a camper trailer was the horse-drawn covered wagon. It was the dominant form of transportation in preindustrial America. The mass production of cars around 1914 led Henry Ford, Thomas Edison, Harvey Firestone, and John Burroughs to embark on a series of camping trips between 1915 and 1924. Their expeditions utilized heavy passenger cars and vans to carry them, their gear, and their staff. By 1919, upwards of fifty vehicles made the journey with them. Ford had designed a car that housed a kitchen with a gasoline stove and built-in icebox. Another vehicle with a truck chassis had compartments for hauling their tents, cots, chairs, electric lights, etc. They even had a round folding table with a lazy Susan that seated twenty people.

The well-organized and well-equipped group called themselves the "Vagabonds" and traveled to destinations like New England's Adirondacks and Green Mountains, and West Virginia, Tennessee, North Carolina, and Virginia. In 1920 they visited John Burroughs's cabin in the Catskill Mountains. By 1924 their now famous camping trips were so popular that the public attention they brought caused them to discontinue their excursions. Before disbanding they gathered at Henry and Clara Ford's Wayside Inn in Massachusetts, and even visited President Coolidge at his home in Vermont.

These cars spotted at a vintage trailer rally are from the same period as the Vagabonds.

The 1920s were a very exciting time. Automobiles were moving rapidly off the assembly lines and regular folks could afford them. Florida was beckoning people from everywhere with its sunshine and the promise of an easy life and good times. Gainesville's businessmen welcomed those regular folks by providing facilities for camping in cars. Not as comfortable as today's campers, but certainly the same idea. People would rig their cars up with folding side tents or convert trucks with sleeping arrangements in the bed of the truck. Camping trailers were being built by craftsmen in their garages, and it wasn't long before commercial trailer production and the formation of camping clubs would launch an industry.

Wally Byam launched his own advertising agency and became the publisher of several magazines. One of his do-it-yourself periodicals included an article describing plans for construction of a travel trailer. After readers complained about the plans, Byam tried them himself and agreed they were flawed. He built his own model—the "Torpedo"—and published an article about the improved trailer, which could be constructed from plywood for less than $100. Byam sold the plans for five dollars and continued building better versions—adding

A Bowlus at the Ride the Wild Surf rally at Newport Dunes in Newport Beach, California. Photo by Hal Thoms Photography.

chemical toilets, iceboxes, gasoline stoves, and hand water pumps. He raised the ceiling to allow campers to stand inside, striving for a trailer, in Byam's words, that would be "always home wherever your wheels may stop." In 1931, Byam's RV company was born; the Airstream name was adopted three years later.

The first aluminum-framed camper trailer, the Bowlus Road Chief, was made in 1934 by Hawley Bowlus at his family ranch in San Fernando, California. Camper trailers have close ties with the aircraft industry's riveted construction methods. As shop foreman at Mahoney-Ryan Airlines, Bowlus supervised the construction of aircraft, including Charles Lindbergh's *Spirit of St. Louis*. With his knowledge of aircraft manufacturing, Bowlus used his expertise to create an aluminum trailer construction design that was later used by Airstream and many other trailer manufactures. In 1936, Byam created one of the first aluminum-bodied Airstream trailers, based on a design by Bowlus. By the late 1930s these small box trailers had evolved into homes on wheels. Units were being produced with full kitchens, flushing toilets, and attractive, detailed designs to meet the needs of couples or families wanting to hit the road or have affordable housing. While many companies built streamlined aluminum travel trailers in the decades to follow, only Airstream has survived to the present day.

Doug Huse and his 1933 Covered Wagon at the Pismo Beach Vintage Trailer Rally.

An early Airstream trailer, ca. 1930s. The man appears to be Wally Byam. This early Airstream trailer is more teardrop shaped than the more recognizable "silver Twinkie" shape that has become iconic. Photo from *Airstream: America's World Traveler*, courtesy of Patrick Foster.

Wally Byam marketed Airstream trailers by demonstrating their prowess as they traveled in large caravans all over the world and caught the public's attention. Airstream eventually became a recognizable American icon associated with "class" and "adventure." Wally sought out tough roads to put his trailers to the test while traveling to the most inspiring locations. The trips were documented with the help of world-class photographers and major magazines like *National Geographic*. Beginning with Wally's tour of postwar Europe in 1948, he partnered with his friend, investor, and fellow trailer enthusiast Cornelius Vanderbilt Jr.

This Studebaker car and trailer look to be of late 1940s vintage. Photo from *Airstream: America's World Traveler*, courtesy of Patrick Foster.

Wally Byam was a good showman and had a great sense of humor. As shown at left, he combined both by showing off two Airstream trailers at once—the larger "Nursery" and smaller "Mother-in-Law." Notice the signs in the windows that point out some of the best features of the sturdy Airstreams. Photo from *Airstream: America's World Traveler*, courtesy of Patrick Foster.

Wally towing a small tandem-axel Airstream with an International pickup. Photo courtesy of Rich Luhr at *Airstream Life* magazine.

Airstreams caravanning as far as the eye can see. Photo courtesy of Rich Luhr at *Airstream Life* magazine.

The trailer they took was a customized Airstream Liner, twenty-two feet long, towed by a hard-cab 1947 CJ-2A civilian jeep that pumped out a mere sixty horsepower. With its low gearing it was functional but agonizingly slow pulling the twenty-two-foot Airstream. There wasn't much point in going fast. Postwar Europe was still in reconstruction, economically depressed, and many of the major cities were still in partial ruin. Among the worst were sections of Germany that had been bombed and were still a war zone under the control of US military forces. Roaming Germany under a US Army travel permit, they drove around bomb craters and saw people still distraught over the recent war activities. Rationed gasoline had to be bought with army coupons.

The three-month trip was a learning experience. The lessons learned then are still applicable to today's vintage trailer enthusiasts, who may face the same challenges as Byam and Vanderbilt did in 1948: limited storage space, carrying capacity, and electrical power. Early Airstreams were extremely light. The twenty-two-foot Liner had interior furniture but not much in the way of appliances. There was no twelve-volt power system (no battery), only a bucket with a lid for a toilet, no holding tanks or hot-water heater. Lighting would have been possible from gas lamps or 120-volt AC power, but European electricity wasn't compatible so Wally and Cornelius made do with the gas lamps. Fresh water was either supplied by a garden hose or in five-gallon jerry cans.

With the two tall men spending three months in a twenty-two-foot trailer, space was at a premium. Wally's general-purpose answer was to ensure that everything they carried could serve three different purposes, and otherwise do without frills. His definition of "frills" included sheets and bedding (sleeping bags would do), flushing toilets, and electricity. Today the very thought of not being able to power rechargeable devices and connect to the Internet at least hourly terrifies many campers, but in 1948 life was in many ways simpler. Wally checked in with the office via telegram or postal mail, so his connectivity tools amounted to paper and pencil, and for the most part when he left the United States nobody expected to hear much until his return.

World War II shifted manufacturing to meet the demands of war. With aluminum on the critical war material list, travel trailer production was put on hold. Following World War II, the returning servicemen and their families needed affordable homes, jobs, and mobility. The camper trailer industry boomed. Such well-known brands as Silver Streak, Alaskan, Dalton, Boles Aero, Kenskill, Shasta, and Aristocrat were all start-up companies during this time. Many were started in garages and empty sheds, while some like Spartan were a response to repurposing their facilities and materials in a postwar economy after having been ramped up to supply a warring nation.

The Arc de Triomphe in Paris is the backdrop for this couple dressed in cowboy outfits. Airstreams traveled the world and got attention wherever they were. Photo from *Airstream: America's World Traveler,* courtesy of Patrick Foster.

Palm Springs Modernism Week

Modernism Week is held each February in Palm Springs, California. The event is a celebration of midcentury modern design, architecture, art, fashion, and culture. It features more than 250 events, including a vintage trailer show, which showcases a collection of trailers, buses, motorhomes, and vintage tow vehicles. Owners are present to talk about their trailers' history and restoration.

Crowds converge on the vintage trailer display at Modernism Week in Palm Springs, California. All photos on pages 36–41 by Hal Thoms Photography.

A 1963 VW Panel Van Sundial Camper conversion with
an original pop-up tent in great condition, owned by
Tony Kadous of Tucson, Arizona.

Hal and Marilyn Thoms's 1953 Aljoa setup.

A 1936 Airstream Silver Cloud, the oldest factory-produced Airstream.

Toni and Chuck Miltenberger's 1936
Airstream and 1937 Chrysler Airflow.

More than fifty trailers are displayed on
blacktop for this Palm Springs event..

There is no shortage of polished
aluminum and rivets.

Midcentury cars like this Edsel wagon
offer a taste of what would have hauled
these coaches back in the day.

From left to right: Airstream, Shasta, Spartan,
and Westcraft trailers.

This 1956 Silver Streak Clipper owned by Frank and Linda Shafer of Arizona won the "Most Original Unrestored" trailer at the Vintage Trailer Show at Modernism Week in Palm Springs, California, in 2017. It includes original flooring, countertops, appliances, bedcovers, and mattresses.

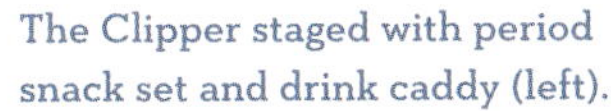

The Clipper staged with period snack set and drink caddy (left).

The United States experienced phenomenal economic growth the decade and a half after World War II. The war brought the return of prosperity, and in the postwar period the United States solidified its position as the world's richest country. More Americans now considered themselves part of the middle class. The automobile and travel trailer industries were partially responsible for this boom. The number of automobiles produced annually quadrupled between 1946 and 1955. A housing boom, stimulated in part by affordable mortgages for servicemen returning from duty, helped fuel the expansion. In the years immediately following World War II, approximately 8 percent of Americans lived in mobile housing. Americans were on the move. Auto and trailer courts, motor lodges, hotels, and trailer parks accommodated them and improved their quality of living while on the road. New highways created better access to once far-away destinations. The Federal-Aid Highway Act of 1956 provided $25 billion, the largest public works expenditure in US history, to create a system of interstate highways linking together all parts of the country. In the postwar period, the West and the Southwest continued to grow—a trend that would continue through the end of the century. Sun Belt cities like Houston, Texas; Miami, Florida; Albuquerque, New Mexico; and Tucson and Phoenix, Arizona, expanded rapidly. Los Angeles, California, moved ahead of Philadelphia, Pennsylvania, as the third largest U.S. city. By 1963, California had more people than New York.

Trail Along to Pismo Vintage Trailer Rally

The first Trail Along to Pismo vintage trailer rally in Pismo Beach, California, was held in May 2008 after a year of planning. It was designed to celebrate the love of vintage trailers and the trailerites who were their caretakers. Cindy and Bob Ross wanted a place where folks from both Northern and Southern California could come together. Cindy found the Pismo Coast Village on the Internet, and worked with original wagon masters Toni and Chuck Miltenberger and Mike Keenan to organize the event. The first year they reserved a hundred sites and feared they wouldn't be able to fill them. But participation exceeded expectations, as 125 trailers showed up that first year.

The early years of the Pismo rally saw trailerites Lynn and Larrie Follstad set up the Saturday morning breakfast at their own expense, Rod and Karinne Olsen provide a night of vintage bowling at the bowling alley in town, Charlie Wallace and Sherry Trochta organize a kite fly, and Chris Hart (later joined by Phil Noyes) present evening movies. After most folks had left on Sunday, those remaining would gather for a "Tumbleweed Get-Together" at Andy Broomhead's site.

After a decade the Pismo rally is still thriving and now hosts 300 vintage trailers, with more on the waiting list trying to get in. The Rosses and Miltenbergers have moved on to start another rally, Cindy Ross' Chula Vista Vintage Trailer Rally in Chula Vista, California.

Beautiful Pismo Beach, California. All photos on pages 44–54 by Hal Thoms Photography, except top right photo on page 49.

This 1937 White Model 706 was one of ninety-eight put into service at Yellowstone National Park between 1936 and 1938.

Rodney Kershaw came all the way from Louisiana to show the Californians his truck-mounted cab over camper. A dilapidated 1950s Airfloat donated its siding and porthole windows to make this camper.

This tent room awning frames a beautiful woody while
acting as a windbreak for the polished vintage Airstream.

This 1957 Corvette and 1950s Ford panel truck belong
to Carlos and Sherry Vivas.

Jerry and Char Appel traveled in their 1937 Yellow Coach (GMC) towing their 1936 Tralette from Lakeside, Montana, to Pismo Beach, California, to meet up with friends at a rally.

A late-1950s DeVille makes good neighbors for this early-1960s Shasta. The Shasta body style was either an Astrodome or an Astroflyte, which were made from 1961 to 1964. The Astrodome model has a toilet; the Astroflyte does not, but still has the forward bump-out bunk.

John and Phyllis Green tow vintage with their air-conditioned early-'50s Chevy pickup. The trailer is a Kamp Master—basically a teardrop trailer with a tent room attachment that you can stand up in.

The ability to express yourself with your trailer design is limitless. This yellow trailer is accented with black trim and the image of a chick wearing a crown. On the front of the trailer, in the upper right corner, it simply says "chirp."

Phil and Ruthie Marler's 1952 Willys Wagon and 1952 Little Caesar, built in Sebastopol, California, by Sokolis Brothers Manufacturing Co.

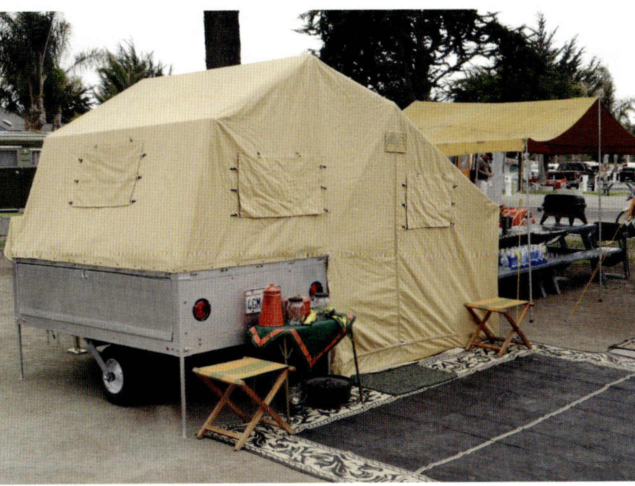

This mid-'60's Heilite is still buttoned up this early in the morning. Heilite Trailers, Inc. was founded by Theodore Heil in 1953 in Lodi, California.

A tent room is a good idea if you are traveling in a teardrop. It's particularly handy for getting dressed without lying down.

A Silver Streak Clipper with the less-common push-out Hehr windows in the front. Most of these models had two fixed oval windows in front that looked good but did not seal well and did not open to provide ventilation.

Originally converted to a fifth wheel in the 1970s, this configuration of a 1951 Spartan was never built in a Spartan factory. Just as beautifully customized is the 1938 Ford COE tow rig.

Robin Sager and Mike Senzamici acquired this 1948 GMC Silversides PD 3751 bus. It was practically new when it was professionally converted to an RV in 1959 by Land Yachts of Egg Harbor, New Jersey, after only ten years of service with Greyhound. By 2010 it was still complete, but run down. It had broken windows and holes in the floor, as well as water leaks and electrical issues. It took about two years and countless hours of work with their two grandsons to restore it to how it was in 1959. It sleeps eight and seats eight at two dinettes. It has a two-person kitchen, and a separate shower and bathroom along with a bedroom in the rear.

A 1959 Streamline in beautiful original condition.

A trolley top truck camper atop a
classic Chevrolet Apache owned
by Scott Burud.

Wally Byam visited Europe, Asia, and Central America numerous times through the midcentury years, each time expanding public awareness of Airstream through massive public relations efforts. He and Cornelius Vanderbilt Jr. continued to travel together occasionally, including such publicity stunts as camping outside the Ambassador East Hotel in Chicago during the Republican and Democratic National Conventions in the 1950s.

In 1951, Wally led a large caravan to Central America that nearly killed him. Sixty-three trailers (not just Airstreams) ventured south of the border. Breakdowns, horrible roads, and extremely difficult conditions caused many of the caravanners to bail out. Eventually, twenty-two trailers made it to the end point at Managua, Nicaragua, and fourteen made the return trip to the United States three months from the day they originally embarked in El Paso. Other trailers were sold, returned by railcar, or stripped for parts and abandoned. Wally lost twenty-seven pounds and picked up a lot of gray hairs. Despite the ordeal, nostalgia about the "exciting" trip set in, and nine months later—quite a bit wiser about caravanning—Wally took off again on a caravan along the west coast of Mexico. And he did it several more times, finally achieving what is probably still the largest trailer caravan ever: 500 trailers in a procession five miles long through Mexico in 1955.

By many estimates, the caravanning adventures under Wally's leadership peaked with the famous Cape Town-to-Cairo caravans, one in either direction, in 1959–60. The ordeal of those trips across parts of Africa that lacked even roads is well documented in back issues of *Airstream Life* magazine (Summer 2006) and *National Geographic* magazine, a documentary movie, and at least two books. The story is as fascinating for the struggles of the participants as it is for the exotic places they visited.

Wally died in 1962. Airstreams had traveled the world, literally, and the world knew it. This became the most potent thing he could have done for his company. Even though the type of caravanning done in the 1950s can hardly be re-created today, the stories and photography that documented it became a legacy.

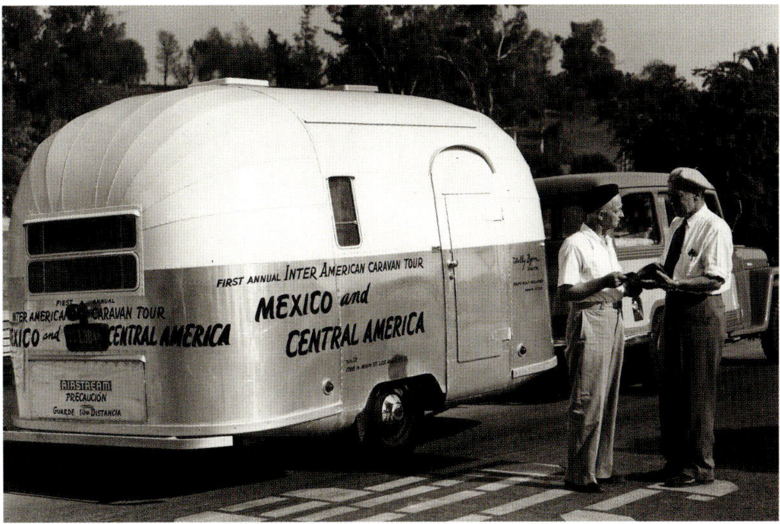

The First Annual Inter-American Trailercoach Caravan Tour to Mexico and Central America. Photo courtesy of Rich Luhr at *Airstream Life* magazine.

An African caravan. The two men on the left are toting rifles for protection against lions and other wild animals. Photo from *Airstream: America's World Traveler,* courtesy of Patrick Foster.

Wally's caravans were well attended and well documented. Many amazing photos remain in the archive to this day. Photo courtesy of Rich Luhr at *Airstream Life* magazine.

Wally Byam made sure that his trailers were seen around the world. Decades later almost anyone can recognize a classic Airstream. Photo courtesy of Rich Luhr at *Airstream Life* magazine.

What could be better than to be with friends camping on the water in your Airstream! (left). San Francisco in 1964, with the Golden Gate Bridge as a backdrop. A 1964 Cadillac is towing an Airstream Land Yacht (right). Photos from *Airstream: America's World Traveler*, courtesy of Patrick Foster.

The camping and road-tripping pastime survived the fuel crisis of the 1970s, and through the last few decades of the twentieth century groups of people continued to get together and enjoy the outdoor lifestyle. Whether in tents, trailers, or motor homes, camping was a means to get together with others who shared common interests. Trips incorporated everything from fishing to motorcycles to dune buggies. Clubs or groups may have been based on the make of RV that you owned or the region where you lived. Just like today, those early wagon masters stepped up to take the lead to organize events and set up rallies.

Traveling to once-distant backwoods became easier following the formation of the US Interstate Highway System. Motor homes grew to forty feet long and had all the comforts of home. Companies like Winnebago began manufacturing on a massive scale. Mass production and competition made the rigs affordable for middle-class America. Fifth-wheel trailers became more popular, offering greater towing stability. Due to the unique hitching system, the overall length of the tow vehicle combined with the length of the trailer was shortened without giving up interior space. The industry was innovative and survived—even thrived—through the economic ups and downs of the next thirty years.

Rallies are a time to have fun and and doll up your site. The awning on this green and white 1953 Fleetwood (above) has a picnic tablecloth pattern against which the red cup lights really pop. Monte Osborn's 1937 Hayes trailer and 1940 Chevrolet (left) are a great color-coordinated pairing. Hayes trailers were all steel, so the modern 302 GMC motor in the Chevy helps pull this small but heavy little trailer down the road. Photos by Hal Thomas Photography.

Billie and Dave O'Neel's Orient Express–Inspired Boles Aero

This 1954 Boles Aero Montecito was built in Burbank, California, and delivered to a ranch family in Wyoming. It was used lightly and then parked in a barn until the elderly widow gave the trailer to her last remaining ranch hand as part of his severance pay when she sold the ranch. He towed the trailer to his hometown of Paris, Texas, and eventually sold it to a man who restored Airstreams as a hobby. He started work on it, but then decided to sell, and the current owners, Dave and Billie O'Neel, purchased it in January 2015. It remained parked in the O'Neels' backyard for a while as they decided what to do with it (much to the dismay of their neighbors).

The eventual design for the trailer's restoration was born out of the O'Neels' twenty-fifth anniversary trip from Venice to Paris aboard the Orient Express—a dream Billie had had for more than twenty years. They loved it so much they decided to recreate the same ambiance in their vintage trailer. They settled on a floor plan that was a mix of the three floor plans originally available for '54 Boles Aero models. It was sectioned into three distinct living spaces: a sitting room, galley, and sleeping compartment. There were twin beds that ran lengthwise from the back end, but they wanted a double bed running sideways to make room for a bathroom.

In addition to the vintage look, they wanted a modern inverter system with the latest technology that could accommodate all the modern conveniences—air-conditioning, a combination water heater, propane and electric heat, holding tanks, onboard water, two flat-screen TVs, and a sound system. All these modern amenities are carefully hidden to prevent clashing with the vintage interior.

Matching blue Samsonite for those spontaneous overnighters.

The O'Neels named their trailer "Wolfi" after their cabin steward on the Orient Express, who saw to their every need while aboard the train.

Achieving the look of the Orient Express was not easy. The O'Neels tried a couple different restoration shops before rolling up their sleeves and diving into the work themselves, along with some help and advice from a carpenter friend. None of the wood paneling was salvageable. They added ceramic tile on the kitchen counter, a material not generally used in vintage trailer restoration. They designed the under-cabinet area and backsplash to float above the stresses of being towed at highway speeds. All the 110-volt lighting is vintage or antique, and they made the draperies and cornices themselves. The embroidered logos on the cornices are from the Orient Express stewards' uniforms. The click-clack sofas are original, as are all the hardware, the kitchen sink, the vent hood above the stove, the windows, the lower kitchen cabinet and drawers, and the lower cabinet in the sitting area known as the California Front, an innovation of Boles Aero. The cabinet tops are covered in onyx tile. The flooring is Marmoleum, set in a period design with an inlaid border.

Billie graciously greeted hundreds of visitors at Modernism Week. She created a clever narrative recording that played inside the trailer explaining some of the trailer's features, its restoration, and interesting facts about the period it was originally built.

This entirely unique crowd-pleaser won the "People's Choice" award at Modernism Week.

The front cabin and dining area. The big window looks out the front of the trailer.

Recalling their dream vacation aboard the Orient Express, Dave and Billie decided they wanted to recreate that same ambiance in their vintage trailer.

The interior is inspired by the look of the dining cars on the Orient Express, including the etched-glass sliding door and the use of Sorrento inlaid wood.

The bathroom is not original to this particular trailer, but was originally available as an option in 1954. The shower curtain, medicine cabinet, and decorative fish are all from the 1950s. There is an antique luggage rack (ca. 1880s) from the New South Wales Railroad in Australia to give the feel of being aboard the Orient Express. The sleeping compartment has a custom headboard designed by Billie that adds storage and hides one of the sound system speakers. The other speakers are hidden under the custom vanity and lower cabinets in the front of the trailer.

The trailer is named "Wolfi" after their cabin steward aboard the train, who remained friends after their trip and helped the O'Neels collect the china and stemware now found in the trailer—the same as is found aboard the train. Wolfi's interior is patterned after the Orient Express's three dining cars: the Etoile du Nord, Côte D'Azur, and L'Oriental. There are accents from each throughout the coach, most notably the use of Sorrento inlaid wood and the etched-glass pocket door.

After two years and countless hours of hard work, Dave and Billie achieved their dream. Billie said Wolfi looks exactly like the original drawings she made while originally sitting in the trailer in their backyard. They are now on the road enjoying their trailer and sharing it with others, as they have traveled from coast to coast aboard their own Orient Express.

It wouldn't be glamping without a chandelier.

The O'Neels took the restoration over the top with the addition of all the antique furniture, making you feel like you are on the Orient Express.

The original stove is a focal point of the kitchen as you pass through from the dining area to the bedroom.

Everywhere you look there is something fun and interesting to see.

This cozy bed is tucked in across
the rear of the trailer, as can be seen
looking in through the rear door.

This bedside table doubles as a vanity.

George Garza's one-of-a-kind camper "Bombs Away" was converted in the 1950s from a B-17 Bomber fuselage. George refurbished this camper as a dedication to his father and other family members that served in the armed forces. Photo by Hal Thoms Photography.

What Is a Vintage Camper Trailer?

The post–World War II construction boom of trailers utilized war surplus aluminum and airplane building techniques along with natural wood interiors. The walls were framed with wood, aluminum, or metal. Breadloaf-shaped trailers from the 1940s like Vagabonds and Westwoods, canned hams like Shastas, Aljos, and Terrys from the '50s, and many other brands being built through the early '60s captured the look and feel that we associate with a vintage camper trailer.

"Ollie T," owned by Michael and Aedan Haworth of Sebastopol, California. Photo by Hal Thoms Photography.

Bob Riggs took these photos with his new camera when he was just a kid in 1952. Mathison Aircraft & Trailer Co., located at 2923 South Street, North Long Beach, California, built two models of Southland trailers: the Runabout and the Pacemaker. Runabouts were from thirteen to eighteen feet long and sold for approximately $100 per foot. Pacemakers ranged from twenty-seven to twenty-nine feet in length and were costlier. Photos by Bob Riggs.

A restored 1950 Westcraft trolley top built by Bob Bergman and Doreen Bailey of Clarkston, Michigan. All photos on this page by Hal Thoms Photography.

An original-condition Westcraft trolley top rescued by Carl and Jaime Holm of the Tinker Tin Trailer Co.

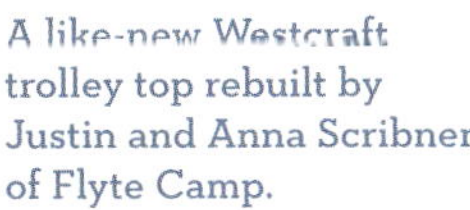

A like-new Westcraft trolley top rebuilt by Justin and Anna Scribner of Flyte Camp.

This five-window 1950 Westcraft Sequoia was restored by Pam and Bob Ambuehl. The trailer was found by chance in the desert outside of Temecula, California, just waiting for the Ambuehls to rescue her.

This 1962 Shasta Airflyte was a crowd pleaser at Modernism Week 2017 in Palm Springs, California. It was completely restored with a distinguished mix of modern amenities and vintage style by designer Randy Gomez of Hollywood Vintage Trailer. All photos on this page by Hal Thoms Photography.

This is a great example of a 1950s canned ham.

Boles Aero Montecito

Scott Burud of Bakersfield, California, outdid himself by blending a 1952 Boles Aero Montecito with a collection of midcentury collectible camping, hunting, and fishing gear. The result was "Arnie's Sporting Goods," a rolling collection of memorabilia displayed in a setting reminiscent of how a sporting goods shop of the 1950s may have looked. It includes such a variety of merchandise that you can get caught up admiring all the items. This trailer is now on display at the Murphy Auto Museum in Oxnard, California. Photos at top of this page and at bottom left on page 73 by Hal Thoms Photography.

SPORTING
CAMPING
HUNTING
FISHING
OPEN
PARKING
IN THE REAR

Facing page: Craig Fraki's trailer displayed at the Ocean Mesa Rally in California. **This page:** Ron and Nancy Roberts's eighteen-foot 1951 Roadmaster. The Robertses have set up a "mailbox" (top right) where friends can leave a note in the event they are out.

* **Aljoa** *

After building several teardrops, Wes and Cindy Nordby from Nevada moved up in size to their 1954 Aljoa Sportsman Model 15. The ground-up restoration of their Aljoa took a year of part-time work to complete. Aljoa travel trailers were first built in Watts, California, in 1945 by C. T. McCreary's Modernistic Industries. The name was changed to Aljo in 1957 following a lawsuit by the similarly named Alcoa (Aluminum Company of America).

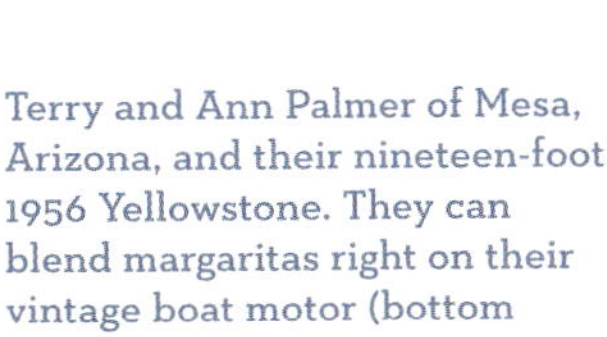

Terry and Ann Palmer of Mesa, Arizona, and their nineteen-foot 1956 Yellowstone. They can blend margaritas right on their vintage boat motor (bottom right).

By the late 1960s the exterior styling of trailers became squarer. The warm amber wood-grain interiors were replaced with lighter imitation wood or pickled white paneling, and were eventually covered with wallpaper-type materials. Late '60s and early '70s colors like avocado green and harvest gold replaced the earlier aqua blues and pinks.

This little trailer has the quintessential "canned ham" shape. Jeff and Brenda Nelson of Corning, California, didn't have to travel far to show their very rare Henslee Lodgette (year unknown) at the Rally at the River at nearby Woodson Bridge State Recreation Area.

Monte Osborn attends the Pismo Beach Vintage Trailer Rally each year to reconnect with friends. He is one of many collectors who brings something new to share from his vast collection each time he attends a rally. Photo by Hal Thoms Photography.

By the 1970s, many trailer manufacturers were no longer in business, and RV brands like Winnebago and Argosy were emerging. Many manufacturers used plastic knobs and trim instead of polished metal latches and natural woods. Handcrafted styling was no longer the standard for the baby-boomer generation. A US economic and gas crisis in the '70s took its toll on both American drivers and RV manufacturers.

An Aljo set up for a pleasant outdoor meal at sunset.

A 1958 Mallard trailer restored by John and Connie Palmer. All photos on this page by Hal Thoms Photography.

A Kenskill restored by Tim and Linda Brown for Monte Osborn (left and above).

✳ *Fireball* ✳

The Rally at the River at Woodson Bridge in Corning, California, was Jeff and Richelle Short's first rally, and not far from their home in Chico, California. Jeff did all the work on their 1968 Fireball himself, with the exception of the exterior paint. His attention to detail is evident in the polishing, fit, and finish that makes this couple's trailer above average. Details like the Fireball hubcaps (top right) are rare and add a nice touch to this clean renovation.

As the vintage trailering hobby matures, the question of what constitutes "vintage" becomes more complicated. In 2015, Shasta built a "reissue" model in the style of a 1962 Shasta Airflyte, with wings included. Other new retro-styled construction trailers and teardrops are also being built on assembly lines by other manufacturers. There are even recent versions of the iconic Holiday House and Trailorboat that are being manufactured new. Smaller operations are hand-building new trailers that *look* like vintage trailers, but have all the modern amenities. Some are custom designs, like the Flyte Camp Neutron. Others are reproductions of actual vintage trailers, like the rare prewar Bowlus trailer. Relic Custom Trailers offers heirloom-quality fiberglass trailers cast from the original molds developed in the 1960s. Individual trailer owners are also building new trailers using old parts like windows, taillights, and fixtures to give their trailer that retro feel. These custom designs incorporate the wildest dreams of a true trailer enthusiast.

At first glance you can't tell you are looking at a brand new Neutron trailer built by Flyte Camp in Bend, Oregon. Photo by Hal Thoms Photography.

Kelly Ross in her 1960s Aristocrat trailer at the Pismo Beach Vintage Trailer Rally in 2017—with enough cake for everyone!

1. Rallies are about the people, the relationships, and the experiences. The trailers are just the reason we get together. We typically have a maximum YOM date of 1972.
2. Custom-built, creative, interesting, unique, well-preserved trailers and RVs from the 1970s through the 1980s may also be admitted to our rallies.
3. Hand-built, heirloom, and custom-built trailers, including teardrop trailers, that closely resemble trailers made prior to 1969 are welcome. These trailers may be built by the owner or a professional shop.
4. Trailers built after 1972 on an assembly line are welcome at our all-inclusive rallies. Often we simply do not have enough space to meet the demand for pre-1972 YOM trailers. A vintage rally or show is appealing because of the era it represents. Having modern trailers mixed into the setting takes away from the vintage atmosphere. Whenever possible, we secure campsites nearby for newer trailers so we can accommodate everyone. (See #1.)
5. Each club, group, or rally will have different guidelines or YOM cutoff dates. The vintage trailer community is very welcoming. Trailers do not have to be fully restored or high-dollar restorations. Come as you are with your project, barn find, or labor of love. You will meet a variety of folks that are willing to help and share their knowledge and experiences with you.

Photo by Hal Thoms Photography.

Jewel

Friends Deb Birdsall and Carolyn Lyman are pictured below with Deb's Jewel (left) and Carolyn's Kenskill (right). These aren't these Tow Girlz' *only* trailers!

More of Deb's pink Jewel.

✳ *Kenskill* ✳

Additional views of Carolyn's Kenskill.

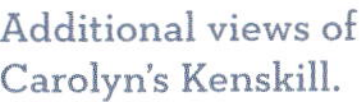

Shasta

CHAPTER 3

The Clubs

"Those who have the cheaper trailers are known as the *Tin Can Tourists*, those who have the elaborate ones are veritable land yachtsman." —*NEW YORK TIMES*, AUGUST 8, 1936

Social media has made finding people with similar interests easier than ever before. Many regions of the United States have their own groups that get together and camp in their vintage trailers. The Trailerettes, Bitches with Hitches, Glamper Gals, and Happy Camper Girls are just a few of the different women's camping groups. Other clubs or groups may be centered around a trailer brand, like the National Serro Scotty Organization or the Wally Byam Airstream Club (WBCCI). Some may be structured, with dues and meetings, while others are just for fun.

TIN CAN TOURISTS

The idea for this pioneering fraternity of auto campers was conceived by James M. Morrison of Illinois, one of the early campers at Desoto Park in Tampa, Florida, in 1919. Morrison created a list of guiding principles for the group:

* To unite fraternally all auto campers.
* To establish a feeling of friendship.
* To provide clean and wholesome entertainment at all meetings.
* To spread the gospel of cleanliness in all camps, as well as help enforce the rules governing all public campgrounds.

Group members could be identified by the soldered tin cans on their radiator caps. Each camper also carried a large assortment of canned goods. There would be cans stashed under the seats, slung over the top, packed along the sides, tucked behind cushions, and stacked on the floor. "They called us Tin Can Tourists, because of our cars and the fact that canned food was frequently on our menus."

New members were inducted through an initiation that included learning the group's secret handshake (performed with a sawing motion), sign (the letter "C" made with the thumb and forefinger), and password (well . . . we can't give away *all* the group's secrets!), and singing the official song, "The More We Get Together," a traditional American folk song whose basic refrain goes like this:

> *The more we get together,*
> *Together, together,*
> *The more we get together,*
> *The happier we'll be.*

> *For your friends are my friends,*
> *And my friends are your friends.*
> *The more we get together,*
> *The happier we'll be.*

Desoto Park, Tampa, Florida, in 1921. At this time there were approximately 17,000 TCT members throughout the United States and Canada.

For the auto camper, the car became the sleeping quarters. Soon companies were selling equipment that could modify a car's seats into sleeping berths. The running boards were often used as headrests.

A Tin Can Tourist camp in Gainesville, Florida. TCT camps were fighting the image of depression-era Hoovervilles and migrants heading to California during the dust bowl, so some parties were turned away and unacceptable behavior was not tolerated. (Hoovervilles, or shantytowns, cropped up across the nation during the depression. Located primarily on the outskirts of major cities, they were named after President Herbert Hoover, who was blamed for the awful economic and social conditions.) The camps were not owned by the TCT, but were developed by the communities to provide camping sites for the visitors from the north. Camp management was often turned over to the TCT.

This 2⅞ inch diameter brass nameplate was recently reproduced by Vintage Trailer Supply in association with Tin Can Tourists. It's very similar to the original prewar TCT badges. In the 1930s, TCT members would mount these on their trailers.

The organization's first meeting was held in Desoto Park in January 1920, and a constitution and by-laws were adopted at a later meeting. The three high points were:

✳ The name: Tin Can Tourists of America
✳ The slogan: "No fees! No Dues! No graft!"
✳ The motto: "Do unto others as you would that they should do unto you."

Little change has been made in the basic principles of the organization since its formation. In 1937 the organization was incorporated, and the word "World" has since been substituted for "America" in the name.

The organization saw a substantial influx of new members during the 1920s and '30s. By the mid-1920s, the locals of Tampa had grown tired of Desoto Park being overrun with the trailerites. In response, the group moved their Winter Convention to Arcadia, Florida, where the community had built a municipal park especially for them.

By 1928–29, the "white-pants Willies" crowd was beginning to take over the Tin Can Tourists, wanting to change the name to "Tin Can Tourists of the World." They dropped the old soup can on the radiator cap, to be replaced by a fancy diamond-shaped radiator emblem that cost you fifty cents.

Pharmaceutical executive Arthur Sherman displayed his Covered Wagon at the Detroit Auto Show in 1930. An old-timer asked Sherman, "You TCT?" Sherman, thinking that might refer to a union, shook his head. The old-timer replied, "You ought to be. If you want to sell these things forget about auto shows and join Tin Can Tourists. Get yourself down to a convention."

A TCT convention in Tampa, Florida, in 1949. This is the area set aside for trailer dealers. Besides being a typical get-together for midcentury trailerites, TCT rallies back in the day had areas where dealers and manufacturers showed their new models. The cars in the photo were likely the vehicles used to pull the trailers, since they all have heavy-duty hitches on the back. These trailers would have been the "new" 1950 models.

By 1930, TCT members were no longer undesirable or considered outsiders and were welcomed into campgrounds and parks. This is the TCT camp in Gainesville, Florida. Other camps were developed in the Florida cities of Jacksonville, Tampa, Arcadia, Sarasota, and Bradenton.

By 1932, membership estimates for the Tin Can Tourists ranged from 30,000 to 100,000. Several communities were actively pursuing the group to host their meets, including the well-attended Winter Convention, which had proven to be an economic boon for the host city. A 250-car caravan led by various Sarasota public officials aided the selection of Sarasota as the 1932 Winter Convention site. Arcadia was chosen as the official site for the group's Homecoming. Less than a decade later, after Sarasota grew tired of the Tin Can Tourists, Tampa offered the Canners a five-year deal to return to Tampa.

By the late '30s the group was hit by a decline in membership due to several factors, including a group of members leaving to form the rival Automobile Tourist Association, a recession in 1939 reducing the number of trailer manufacturers, and the beginning of World War II.

Breadloaf-style trailers were built from the late 1930s through the 1940s.

In 1948, some members tried changing the name to "Trailer Coach Tourists." There was another attempt to change the club's name in 1959—some claiming that the name "Tin Can" connoted a certain cheapness. The proposed new name was "Twentieth Century Tourists of the World," but even though a plurality of members favored the name change, the vote lacked a necessary two-thirds majority.

In 1949 the club reportedly had 80,000 members (up from 30,000 a decade earlier). In 1963 the membership was 100,000. The club continued to host events across the eastern United States through the mid-1970s, but by the mid-'80s the club no longer existed.

In 1998, Forrest and Jeri Bone revived the club as an all-make-and-model vintage trailer and motor coach club. The renewal gathering was held in May 1998 at Camp Dearborn in Milford, Michigan. Twenty-one rigs attended that first gathering, and by the end of that year fifty charter members had been accepted to the new version of the Tin Can Tourists. The group has grown steadily, holding annual gatherings in Michigan and Florida, and regional rallies at various locations in the United States.

The Bones are the club directors, with help from regional representatives to develop TCT activities in their areas. Regional representatives have also been added in England, Japan, and France.

The new version of Tin Can Tourists is open to all. Its goal is to abide by the original group's objectives. TCT offers its members a chance to meet and have fun with other owners who share their interest in vintage RVs. You don't have to own a vintage trailer or motor coach to participate. There are several members, including charter members, who come every year to the annual gathering who do not currently own a vintage rig.

Website: tincantourists.com

Maurrie Sussman and Becky Clarke were having so much fun fishing in Montana they decided to invite some of their girlfriends along on their next trip. That's how Sisters on the Fly was born. All photos on pages 90–96 by Ceci Bennett.

SISTERS ON THE FLY

Sisters on the Fly began on a fishing trip in Montana in August 1999. Sisters Becky Clarke and Maurrie Sussman were celebrating the day's catch (and release) back at camp with a glass of wine when they got to thinking, "We are having way too much fun to keep all the good times to ourselves. Let's invite some of our girlfriends to come along on the next trip."

SOTF has grown from two sisters on a trout fishing excursion to over 8,000 registered members—what has become the largest women's outdoor adventure organization in the country.

Sisters Becky and Maurrie were brought up by their adventurous mother, Mazie, who taught them how to enjoy the outdoors and become capable, independent women. Mazie lived to be ninety-four and her spirit is still with her daughters as they continue to inspire women to travel, camp, fish, and explore every horizon as empowered adventurers.

Maurrie (right) and Becky (left), SOTF sister Nos. 1 and 2, with a 1963 Shasta trailer outfitted with period fishing gear.

Happy campers Becky and Maurrie with "Amazing Mazie," named after their mother, Mazie. It's painted in a bold, nontraditional, themed paint scheme that is common among members of SOTF. Many go with a Western or fishing theme, but anything goes. Sisters often proudly tout their association with SOTF by displaying their membership number and the group's logo on their trailers.

SOTF's stated mission is "Offering empowerment and sisterhood through exceptional outdoor adventures," with the goal of challenging women in all that they set their minds to. All women twenty-one years or older who want to share in the adventures of sisterhood are welcome.

A Sister on the Fly does not need to own a trailer or have any special camping, fishing, or other particular skills to join. Those that *do* own trailers may own a vintage or not-so-vintage trailer. Many of the SOTF trailers and RVs are easy to spot. Themed murals adorn many of the exteriors with hand-painted graphics that speak to the owner's style. Sisters also show their sisterhood with their SOTF member number painted on their rig.

"We have more fun than anyone" is their credo, as they socialize, mobilize, and recreate together. Members learn to fish, ride a horse, kayak, camp under the stars, and travel to various destinations near and far. The best part of Sisters on the Fly is simply meeting new sisters, like-minded and kindred spirits.

There is one rule for Sisters on the Fly events and outings: "No Men, No Kids, Be Nice, Have Fun!"

The interior of this SOTF trailer features campy, chic décor, including cowboy hats, Mexican blankets, and pillows adorned with fish and a vintage trailer.

Lace, floral patterns, and quilts create a comfy backdrop for the antiques displayed in this bright and airy vintage trailer.

Marty Knight, sister No. 669,
named her vintage Aladdin trailer
"Dilly Dally Sally."

This "Cowgirl Tough" trailer was auctioned off by Sisters on
the the Fly to benefit Casting for Recovery, a unique retreat
program that strives to enhance the quality of life for women
with breast cancer. The program combines fly fishing with
breast cancer education and peer support.

Teresa Klocke, sister No. 430, proudly proclaims on the side of her trailer, "I took to makin' trouble like most women take to makin' biscuits!" The trailer is also adorned with vintage Zane Grey movie posters against the backdrop of a faux wood paint scheme on its vintage aluminum exterior. Grey was best known for his popular novels that idealized the notion of the simple, adventurous lifestyle of the Old West.

The interior of Becky Clarke's "Cowgirl Camp" trailer. Playing in the great outdoors doesn't mean you have to be uncomfortable.

A fireplace makes this a cozy retreat when you're roughing it.

The clean and brightly painted interior of this trailer includes a Western touch with horseshoes used for handles on the cupboards and drawers.

This vintage trailer, more than twenty feet in length and sixty-plus years old, can't hide in the wild with its turquoise paint and Native American–themed mural. The interior, warmed by the patina wood finish, provides a Southwestern cabin feel.

Elaine Martin's 1965 Airstream Caravel displays some of her vast collection of period-correct camping gear. A longtime collector of vintage items, Elaine bought and towed her first trailer less than a decade ago and has embraced the hobby ever since. She's owned several trailers and traveled thousands of miles across the United States over the past several years. Photos by Ingrid Nelson.

Member-hosted events and special destination trips run the gamut from camping to fishing, hiking, horseback riding, wine tasting, line dancing, and whatever else sounds like fun to the members.

In 2015, Becky became vice president and a founding member of the board of directors of the Mazie Morrison Foundation. Maurrie serves as president of SOTF and president/chairman of the board of the Mazie Morrison Foundation. The foundation is dedicated to supporting women and children in their endeavors to succeed in any capacity, as represented and inspired by the spirit of Becky and Maurrie's mother, Mazie.

CHRISTIAN VINTAGE TRAILER CLUB

Founded in 2009 by David and Karen Jennings, the club is dedicated to the love of vintage trailers and the Lord. The CVTC is based in Southern California and hosts the annual Ride the Wild Surf vintage trailer rally at Newport Dunes in Newport Beach, California. The rallies include a pizza party Friday night, continental breakfasts Saturday and Sunday, an open house on Saturday (open to the public), ice cream social, potluck, movies, and more. Based in Southern California, CVTC welcomes everyone.

Website: www.facebook.com/groups/54726617935/

Classic tow vehicles come in all shapes and sizes. Photos by Hal Thoms Photography.

Fun at a Ride the Wild Surf Vintage Trailer Rally at Newport Dunes, Newport Beach, California. Photos by Hal Thoms Photography. Image of logo below provided by Christian Vintage Trailer Club.

A classic teardrop-style trailer. All
photos on pages 100–01 by Hal Thoms
Photography.

ROLLIN' OLDIES VINTAGE TRAILERS

The group began in July 2007 in conjunction with an open car show near Salem, Oregon. Eighteen vintage trailers attended the first outing, an informal meeting was called, the idea of forming a vintage trailer group was discussed, and ROVT was born. Founders Jerry and Linda Kwiatkowski, from Dallas, Oregon, have dedicated ten years to making ROVT the Northwest's largest vintage trailer group.

Jerry and Linda formed ROVT with the intention of not having to deal with politics like they did in several car clubs they had formed previously. They decided early on that ROVT would *not* have club meetings, officers, dues, or a formal organization.

All ROVT rallies are hosted by volunteers, who give their time to organize events in Oregon, Idaho, California, and Washington State. At any given time there may be eight or nine rallies on the calendar in the Pacific Northwest. Most of the rallies are held in state parks and a rally fee of ten dollars is collected to offset expenses like liability insurance, decals, and open/closed signs. None of the volunteers, including the founders, are paid. Any extra money from the site collections is used to fund future rallies.

In 2009 they found a much bigger park near Sweet Home, Oregon, called Sunnyside Park. All twenty-eight campsites in the group area were filled, and they had a waiting list in case there were any cancellations. In 2010, the group found River Bend Park, located a few miles down the road on the banks of the South Santiam River. Currently they reserve seventy sites and rent them to the members so they have control over making River Bend a true vintage trailer rally, with no RVs newer than 1980.

The River Bend rally held in June is the flagship of the group's rallies and is usually sold out a year in advance. The beautiful park draws a lot of participants, with a waiting list of over fifty additional campers hoping for a cancellation.

Website: www.rovt.org

Image of logo provided by Rollin' Oldies Vintage Trailers.

Vintage collections on display at an ROVT gathering in Oregon.

Eric Sande purchased his 1950 Traveleze project in 2010. A true canned ham, he had to have it. Eric assumed he could do the work necessary to make it camp-worthy, but quickly decided he needed professional help. He called a new start-up company called Flyte Camp, which was confident it could get the trailer back on the road. Once in the shop, it didn't take long to realize the wood rot was extensive and the trailer would need a complete frame-off restoration.

The restored trailer is authentic to its original design, however Flyte Camp did manage to squeeze in a few modern conveniences, such as instant hot water and AC (hidden in the closet and under the bed, respectively). The finished product is spectacular and the legacy of this little canned ham will hopefully live on for another sixty-five years.

TOW BOYZ AND TOW GIRLZ VINTAGE CAMPER TRAILERS CLUBS

For several years we attended rallies and car shows and were constantly asked if we were a club. Eventually we decided maybe it would be easier to say yes than to explain that we were just a bunch of friends who liked to camp together in our old trailers. If the car guys had a club, why couldn't we? We came up with Tow Boyz out of reverence for a local car club called the Poor Boys. It didn't take long for the women to want their own club, and so Tow Girlz was born. Since it was all just for fun, we encouraged others to start their own chapters in their region. We've laid the groundwork with T-shirts, decals, and a website. To join, all you have to do is to find a chapter near you (or start one) and purchase a T-shirt. We will help you organize, promote, and plan rallies.

Website: www.towboyz.com or www.towgirlz.com

FAMILY MOTOR COACH ASSOCIATION

The Family Motor Coach Association was founded in 1963 by several RVing families in Hinckley, Maine. When the group was formed, RVs were not as readily available as they are today. Imaginative RVers converted school buses, transit buses, bread trucks, and similar types of vehicles into RVs. Today the membership is at more than 71,000 motorhome-owning families. With the RV industry's growth in recent years, the association's membership continues to grow. FMCA has held RV rallies since its formation. Currently they host two conventions a year in varying locations throughout the United States. These events are open to towable-trailer owners as well as FMCA members.

Website: www.fmca.com

Logo image courtesy of Family Motor Coach Association.

NO VACANCY
PIERRE & LAURENCE'S
Airstream
Guest House
CALIFORNIA
US
66

WALLY BYAM CARAVAN CLUB INTERNATIONAL

As one of the founding members of the Wally Byam Caravan Club International, Helen Byam Schwamborn—WBCCI member No. 2—established the first WBCCI headquarters office and served as the first editor of the club newsletter, the *Blue Beret*. Today, WBCCI members continue to travel in style with their Airstreams each year on dozens of national and international caravans, and enjoy camping with new and old friends at the hundreds of local, regional, and special event rallies. Founded in 1955 by 39 charter members, the WBCCI today is one of the largest recreational vehicle organizations in the world, with more than 12,000 members. The WBCCI has touched the lives of Airstream owners for decades and continues in the spirit of Wally Byam, the inventor of the Airstream, who introduced glamour to trailer travel. Dedicated to fostering friendships and a passion for travel through a common interest in Airstreams, the WBCCI offers caravans, rallies and activities through the more than 122 local units throughout the United States and Canada. The WBCCI is a nonprofit organization, directed by volunteer members. A minimal paid staff manages the WBCCI headquarters in Jackson Center, Ohio.

Airstream trailers have survived millions of miles over some of the roughest roads in the world, realizing Wally Byam's dream as stated in his well-known creed. "In the heart of these words is an entire life's dream," he wrote. "To those of you who find in the promise of these words, your promise, I bequeath this creed . . . my dream belongs to you."

Website: wbcci.org

Pierre Bogros is the owner and the designer of this custom, fully restored 1971 Airstream. Photo by Paul Barnaby.

The Wally Byam Creed

To place the great wide world at your doorstep for you who yearn to travel with all the comforts of home.

To provide a more satisfying, meaningful way of travel that offers complete travel independence, wherever and whenever you choose to go or stay.

To keep alive and make real an enduring promise of high adventure and faraway lands . . . of rediscovering old places and new interests.

To open a whole world of new experiences . . . a new dimension in enjoyment where travel adventure and good fellowship are your constant companions.

To encourage clubs and rallies that provide an endless source of friendships, travel fun, and personal expression.

To lead caravans wherever the four winds blow . . . over twinkling boulevards, across trackless deserts . . . to the traveled and untraveled corners of the earth.

To play some part in promoting international goodwill and understanding among the peoples of the world through person-to-person contact.

To refine and perfect our product by continuous travel-testing over the highways and byways of the world.

To strive endlessly to stir the venturesome spirit that moves you to follow a rainbow to its end . . . and thus make your travel dreams come true.

Airstream Cruiser

Scotty and Vanessa Williams had some fun with this 1954 Airstream Cruiser before it found a new home. Scotty and Vanessa own Artistic Airstreams Inc., a vintage trailer restoration company in Concord, California, that stays busy customizing and restoring Airstreams as well as other vintage trailers. This example of their work was sold to an international buyer. All photos on pages 110-11 by Dale Godfrey.

GOOD SAM CLUB

In 1966, a reader of *Trail-R-News* wrote a letter to the publisher with a suggestion for a new club. The idea for the club was based on the principles outlined in the biblical story of the Good Samaritan. The publisher liked the idea and had stickers of a smiling, haloed mascot printed for club members to affix to their trailers. If a member saw another member stranded on the side of the road, they were encouraged to stop and help them.

At about the same time, an RV park store in Kentucky named Camping World was selling camping gear to those who enjoyed the outdoor lifestyle. When *Trailer Life* magazine publisher Art Rouse purchased *Trail-R-News,* the Good Sam Club was included as part of the deal. Eventually, RV park discounts and other benefits were added as perks of being a member of the Good Sam club. In 1997, the club's parent company joined forces with Camping World, which by that time had grown into a large retail chain. Today, the chairman and CEO of Camping World and Good Sam Enterprises, Marcus Lemonis, strives to take both companies to the next level. Good Sam Club benefits have expanded and their membership continues to increase.

Website: www.goodsamclub.com

BOLER BITCHES

Boler Bitches (not to be confused with Bitches with Hitches) is a club for individuals who are crazy for Boler trailers and other vintage campers. Bolers are fiberglass trailers manufactured in Winnipeg, Manitoba. If you simply want to enjoy the fun and friendship of other likeminded people, this is the club for you. The club's slogan is, "You'll never be homeless as long as you own a camper."

Website: bolerbitches.com

You don't have to be in a club to have fun at a vintage trailer rally. This crew is doing just fine at the Pismo Rally in Pismo Beach, California. Photo by Hal Thoms Photography.

Founder Amanda Hoppe (Boler Bitch No. 001), from Red Deer, Alberta, named her 1973 1300 series Boler trailer "Rusty B" (above and page 113).

Amanda Shumack and Bill Moeller

Amanda Shumack and Bill Moeller refurbished their first vintage trailer, a 1969 Shasta Loflyte, in a whimsical style that reflected their artistic side. The purple upholstered chairs were modified by removing the rear legs so they could sit on top of the fender wells.

Amanda and Bill have been avid vintage trailerites for less than two years and have already bought their next vintage camping rig, a 1960 International Harvester B110 series. It's a half-ton heavy-duty truck. The first owner, John Erickson, special ordered it from the International Harvester Company and had it exported to Longview, Washington, in 1960. He custom-built the camper over a period of three years. Once the build was completed he took the truck camper on a road trip to Alaska and Canada. Because it was custom built, this is the only registered IH truck camper known to exist. The camper only changed hands a couple of times before ending up in the care of Amanda and Bill.

Photo by Peter Holderness.

Yes, we really camp in them! Smoke from the morning campfire drifts across a herd of Boles Aeros.

Rally Types

Vintage trailerites participate in several different types of get-togethers. Each event is unique, based on the host's plans, the park's amenities, and other attractions in the area. This chapter is a guide to the diverse types of rallies we have either attended or hosted. Most rallies will not follow just one type to the letter. Take ideas that you like from each different format to create an event that sounds like fun and that you can manage.

Rallies are not only filled with vintage trailers, they also attract a variety of classic cars. Photo by Hal Thoms Photography.

RALLIES

A vintage trailer rally is an opportunity for like-minded individuals, referred to as trailer-ites, to get together to camp, eat, and socialize with others who have a common interest in preserving the past. A vintage trailer rally may establish a maximum year of manufacture (YOM) date. This date can range from the early seventies to the early eighties, depending on the event. Trailers manufactured after the established date may not be admitted to some events unless they are of some special interest or limited production, or a custom creation that would have widespread appeal.

Randy and Charmaine Bonfantini took their newly self-restored 1955 Lakewood and started a rally at Manchester Beach, California, in 2015. The well-attended rally, with about forty trailers, has sold out each year.

Interior views of
Randy and Char's
1955 Lakewood.

We meet at a campground on a Thursday or Friday as our personal lives permit. Reservations are made up to a year in advance to secure a site with the amenities that our trailers require. Some campgrounds offer sites with everything from full hookups (water, electric, septic, and cable TV), to water and electric only, and just dry camping (no hookups). Electrical service can range from 15 amps to 30 amps or 50 amps. A small canned ham trailer with minimal electrical needs will function off a 15-amp electrical hookup, whereas a larger RV with air-conditioning may need the 50-amp service. Be sure you know your electrical requirements and have a variety of plug adapters available to connect to the different outlets at the parks that you will visit. Other options for power could include generators, solar panels, or 12-volt batteries. A septic hookup is useful if you have a toilet or shower in your trailer. If you are only using a small sink, a portable wastewater container will likely suffice for several days. Other considerations when making your reservations may include requests for shade, the proximity to a restroom, or accessibility requirements that you may have regarding hills or uneven surfaces that you may be camping on (if you have limited mobility, or use a wheelchair or other walking aids, you may need to know these things so you can plan for them).

Friends from Oregon have customized personal mobility scooters into attention-getting transportation.

A huge fire pit at the Manchester Beach campground makes a good place for everyone to get together in the evening. Cool coastal weather makes a raging fire necessary for warmth, and good for toasting marshmallows and cooking wadingers!

These ladies took time from their tea at Trailerfest 2016, Christmas in the Trailer Park, to pose for a group photo.

A rally may include a potluck dinner or an appetizer party. We like to have one of these on the first night of the rally, usually a Thursday. It's a great time for everyone to get together and say hello while they break bread. Having this event on the first night seems to make it easy for people to bring a fresh dish to contribute to the meal. On Friday the rest of the trailers arrive and everyone either reacquaints themselves with old friends or welcomes the newbies. The rest of the weekend may include anything from campfires to watching vintage movies to an open house. Each rally is different in how many and what kind of events are planned for the weekend. Some, like Trailerfest in Lodi, California, are jammed full of live bands, food, and classic cars. Others, like the Fallen Leaf Lake Rally in South Lake Tahoe, California, offer a serene campground with little to no planned activities. Both types of rallies are enjoyable and offer a variety of experiences that will suit everyone.

Campers potluck at the Trailers in the Trees rally at Smithwoods RV Park, nestled in the redwoods in the Santa Cruz Mountains, Felton, California.

Hal and Marilyn Thoms's campsite at dusk at the Ride the Wild Surf rally at Newport Dunes. Their Studebaker pickup drags their 1953 Aljoa to several rallies each year. Hal contributed many of the photos in this book, as well as to *Vintage Camper Trailers* magazine. Photo by Hal Thoms Photography.

A 1951 Spartan set up as a rental at
La Siesta Campgrounds in Arivaca,
Arizona.

A Beemer trailer.

A chili cook-off at La Siesta Campgrounds.

Halloween-themed decorations.

BOONDOCKING

This format works for a casual campout or a full-blown rally. This type of event can be held just about anywhere that you can park trailers. Public parks, fairgrounds, or private residences that have space can host this kind of trailer get-together. Trailer owners are invited to park within a designated area, anywhere and however they like. Circle the wagons with your friends or find a remote spot under the shade of some trees. These events are usually not held at regular campgrounds, so they are dry camping with little or no hookups. Sometimes limited electrical or water may be available on site. There needs to be arrangements made for restroom facilities or portable toilets. Shower facilities may be even harder to come by at these events. Fairgrounds often have showers on the property. If it is a summer event near water, you may just need to get back to nature and take a dip. Most of the smaller vintage trailers don't have much in the way of hookups, so roughing it for a couple of days can be fun. Quiet generators that respect other campers' privacy and quiet times are also options to recharge cell phones or use other electrical appliances as needed. We boondock at the All-American Vintage Trailer Rally in Brooks, Oregon, for the Fourth of July. The event is held on the grounds of Powerland Heritage Park, and a Civil War reenactment group takes up the rest of the park on the same weekend. It is quite a weekend of vintage trailering combined with a bugle reveille every morning and cannons blasting in the distance. Both groups appreciate the other's effort and the energy that goes into respecting and preserving these distinctly different periods of America's past.

Boondocking at Powerland Heritage Park in Brooks, Oregon.

More scenes from Powerland Heritage Park, Brooks, Oregon.

OPEN
1960
RELIC
Vintage Trailers
Mon-Fri By
Appt. Only
253-431-9709

Above: Thom Underwood boondocking in his Thom Thumb trailer. The trailer is based on a 1950 Rod and Reel trailer. This new build is handcrafted by Thom but stays faithful to the original designs and materials of its predecessor. **Facing page:** Boondocking doesn't mean you have to cut back on your decorations.

CAMPOUTS

A campout is a casual get-together with no host, no rally fees, and very few activities. A campout can be just a few friends, or a few dozen trailerites getting together. Each camper usually makes their own reservation with the campground. These outings can be held at a campground, private residence, winery, or just about anywhere you can park your trailer. A campout is the easiest type of rally to organize because it is just camping and does not require planned activities. Simply pick a date, pick a location, and let your trailer friends know your plans. If you have enough room, let your friends know to invite their friends. Social media, *Vintage Camper Trailers* magazine (www.vintagecampertrailers.com), and local trailer clubs can also be resources to put the word out about your campout. Keep it casual. Sometimes it's OK just to get together with no plans, no timelines, and no concerns about getting set up for an open house.

A campout can be a good get-together for a large group of friends on a holiday weekend, especially for those that might otherwise spend the holiday alone. Not everyone can attend every year because of other commitments, but being with friends is preferred by most as opposed to spending a holiday alone. We have attended rallies on Easter, both Mother's and Father's Day, as well as New Year's celebrations. These have been great casual campouts with friends when other family commitments didn't interfere. Always make sure to give people plenty of time to plan by announcing your campouts many months in advance.

Gary and Linda Woodward with their dog, Darla, in front of their 1956 Silver Streak.

Darla dressed to the nines.

A private residence works for a casual campout. Events that are not held on regular campgrounds are usually dry camping and have little or no hookups.

The one-acre Woodward Farm in Riverside, California, has hosted a Valentine's Day campout for about a dozen trailers for the past four years. Hosts Gary and Linda Woodward open their home to their trailerite friends.

All the women (Darla included!) sported pink
flamingo jammies just in case there was a photo op at
the Valentine's Day campout at Woodwrd Farm. Looks
like it paid off!

Gilbert and Sharon Leon from Highland, California,
with their 1960 Kenskill.

Christopher Baas and Cheryl Swain from Riverside,
California, with their 1957 Westerner.

Thom and Marian Butler from Riverside, California,
with their 1969 Serro Scotty.

Vintage trailerites caravan from a predetermined meeting place, through the town of Petaluma, California, to the campground.

CARAVANS

In Europe, trailers are commonly referred to as "caravans." In the United States, a "caravan" is more frequently used to describe a group of RVs traveling together. Getting there can be half the fun! You can caravan to a planned event, such as a rally or campout, or come up with a route that you and several other friends can travel together. Either way, be sure to have planned stops along the way. Invariably people will need fuel, food, and bathrooms. Stopping to stretch and see the sights will make the trip more pleasant for everyone. Consider limiting the size of your group If you are planning a caravan as an event. Travelers in the caravan may all meet up at the beginning of the trip or join the group along the way, if the planned stops and overnights have been predetermined. Depending on the time your group can allot for the trip, you may spend anywhere from one night to a few nights in each location seeing the sites and experiencing what the area has to offer.

The rally in Petaluma, California, each year puts a twist on the caravan concept. Trailers congregate across town from the campground at a predetermined time. When it is time to depart, the trailers file out and go through the old town of Petaluma. With a dozen or more vintage trailers being towed by a variety of classic cars and modern tow vehicles, it is quite a spectacle that gets many looks, photographs, and thumbs up by the unsuspecting shoppers in town that morning. The campground is aware that several of us will be checking in at the same time and makes arrangements to accommodate our congested arrival.

Just about anything goes at a rally!

Rosa Sanchez, beautifully outfitted and lending to the atmosphere of the rally's theme, shows her rally spirit at Trailerfiesta. Photo by Stan Drury.

Wayne and Kathy Ferguson host dinner for the gang outside their 1955 Aljoa.

Paul, Caroline, Grace, and Angelo Lacitinola stop by the WestHaven Senior Living home in Orland, California, on the way to the Rally at the River at Woodson Bridge.

For the past few years, on our way to a rally at Woodson Bridge in Corning, California, we stop by an assisted living facility so the residents there, who cannot travel, can enjoy seeing the trailers they grew up with. We invite other rally attendees to make the stop with us. The facility generously provides us lunch. The residents tell us about their camping adventures when they were camping in the trailers that we now collect. Taking the time to do this is as much for our benefit as it is for theirs. Making sure that our children connect with the older generation is important to us. Hearing their stories about their families, their camping trips, and their trailers reinforces to us how important your memories are—forever.

DISPLAY SHOWS

Organizers of car shows, antique fairs, and other public events are aware of the public appeal of vintage trailers. We are invited to bring our trailers to more events than we can possibly attend each year. The vintage trailers are a draw to admirers and dreamers that may not own a vintage trailer but can appreciate them either for their design or level of restoration. Some attendees may be looking to purchase a trailer while others are just spending time reminiscing. It's not just the collectors and restorers that love the old tin. Vintage trailer displays can be used to round out an existing event or as a stand-alone event where visitors pay an admission price to view the display. We participate with our vintage trailers at fundraising shows at Palm Springs Modernism Week, the Murphy Auto Museum in Oxnard, California, and Bothe-Napa Valley State Park near Calistoga, California. The public pays an entrance fee to tour the trailers at each of these events to the benefit of the host organization.

Classic midcentury cars and trailers share the spotlight at Palm Springs Modernism Week.

At some of the events we stay in our trailer overnight, but others require us to stay in a nearby hotel if the display area doesn't allow camping. Many times these types of events are by invitation only. If you have the opportunity to participate, be prepared to spend the day chatting with hundreds of people about your trailer and its restoration. We like to prepare some signage that gives the public some basic details about the trailer. This will help reduce your need to repeat some of the basic information over and over again. We include things like year, make, model, length, weight, what it may have cost new, and other interesting facts surrounding its date of manufacture, how long the restoration took, your hometown, etc. An 8.5 x 11 inch laminated sheet works well. One of the neatest things I've seen recently is a looped audio presentation played over the stereo system in a beautifully restored Boles Aero trailer. The owner, Billie O'Neel, did the narration and shared interesting facts about the trailer's manufacture and restoration.

My advice is to jump at the chance to participate in these types of events if you like meeting new people and speaking with the public. Do not commit to participate in an event like this unless you are sure you can attend. Find out the details like set-up time, show hours, what hookups are available, and if you can stay in your trailer overnight. Another detail you may not think of is the kind of surface where the trailer will be parked. If you are not on dirt or grass and want to set up an awning, you will need to consider how you will anchor the awning without driving stakes into the ground. If you are displaying your trailer at a fundraising event there should be little or no cost to you. Each event varies in how it is structured financially, but this also needs to be clear and agreed upon in advance.

Planning this type of event may require some experience or help in dealing with all the logistics involved. Unless you have planned public events in the past, you may need to enlist the help of someone who has. Events like this may require insurance, permits, and marketing, just to name a few things, that are not typical to a camping-type rally (see Chapter 5: How to Host a Rally).

Shasta
18

Facing page: Preparing for a day of interaction at Palm Springs Modernism Week. **This page:** After dark is a favorite time at any rally. All photos by Hal Thoms Photography.

A parking lot show at the
Murphy Auto Museum in
Oxnard, California.

BOOT CAMP

This event is very different from typical rallies, shows, and other types of get-togethers. Modeled after its predecessor, the Vintage Trailer Academy, Boot Camp is an opportunity for trailerites to get together and learn the best practices for restoring old trailers. Vintage Trailer Academy, last held in 2014 in Albuquerque, New Mexico, primarily dealt with the building practices used on Airstream trailers. With Boot Camp, we wanted to include a more general approach for all makes and models. Beginning in 2016 we have held our Boot Camp events in Northern California. Attendees travel from all over the United States to attend a variety of seminars presented by professionals and experts in their field of restoration. By holding these events at a campground, attendees can bring their vintage trailers, camp in their newer RVs, or rent a cabin on-site. Boot Camp is as much about the contacts and camaraderie created as it is about the seminars and what you will see and experience. Planning this type of event is complicated and the most logistically intense. Our plans include more Boot Camps at different locations and advanced courses that go more in depth for trailerites who want to do it themselves.

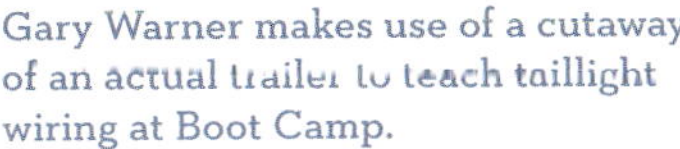
Gary Warner makes use of a cutaway of an actual trailer to teach taillight wiring at Boot Camp.

Jenny, Linda, and Faye-bulous are part of the behind-the-scenes crew it takes to keep things running smoothly at Boot Camp.

Above: Jimmy Evans doesn't just tell you how to paint a trailer, he shows you! **Facing page:** Bonnie Roberts was one of many women who attended Boot Camp 2017 in their own trailer. Her pink 1963 Shasta is an eye-catcher.

Deborah Maddock's 1950 Aljoa Sportsman.

Harp's RV Service from Lincoln, California, stayed in their vintage Traveleze (top) and set up shop just outside (above).

Vintage trailers come in all shapes and sizes. These owner/builders brought their trailers to Boot Camp 2017 in Lodi, California (pages 146–47).

Tim and Linda Brown's 1959 Trailfeather

Tim and Linda Brown's latest project is a 1959 Trailfeather. This unique trailer has a lever on the front that actuates a drop-down section of the floor right inside the doorway. The floor lowers all the way to the ground, allowing more headroom to stand between the dining area (which makes into a bed) and the galley. The painted canvas tent room is original to the trailer.

TRAIL FEATHER

BRAND- OR TYPE-SPECIFIC

Popular trailer brands have a very loyal fan base. Prolific manufactures like Airstream, Spartan, Boles Aero, Streamline, Aristocrat, Serro Scotty, and Shasta have an almost cult-like following among their owners. Manufacturers themselves, or brand-loyal owners, may host rallies for one specific brand or a particular type of trailer. Owners of the 2015 reproduction or reissue 1962 Shastas even hold rallies for their newly manufactured, vintage-styled trailers. Rallies featuring teardrop, tent, and fiberglass trailers are examples that focus more on the design of the trailer than any particular brand. Rallies with as narrow a scope as this will often allow other vintage trailers to participate even though they may not exactly match the event's theme. Rallies may also choose to target a specific era or decade, allowing only trailers that were manufactured within a certain range of years to attend. If you are a fan of a certain brand or specific type of trailer, this sort of rally will be right up your alley.

A 1955 Starfire.

Gypsy Time Travelers

At a recent Vintage Camper Trailers Boot Camp event we had the Gypsy Time Travelers and their rig, "Florence." Husband and wife Michael Olson and Christy Horne converted a modern Freightliner FL60 cab into an RV, complete with a stage, castle turrets, and a blacksmithing shop! Michael is an eccentric builder, a master blacksmith, and a welder and woodworker extraordinaire. Michael and Christy travel to events and deliver a stage show they describe as "fabulous storytelling with live anvil accompaniment."

The couple named Florence after Christy's grandmother because she was one of the few people who supported them and their unique job choices over the decades. Florence has two 8 x 8 foot loft-style bedrooms upstairs in telescoping turrets. Michel and Christy's bedroom is called the Captain's Quarters. The second bedroom, which functions as an attic, is called the Pirate's Lounge. Florence is built of wood and iron, and has twenty-three portholes, giving it the look of a ship with pirate salvage overtones. Huge chains hold up the three drawbridge stages/porches, which Michael made.

Florence has everything the couple needs to live on the road seven to nine months out of each year: a kitchen with refrigerator, generator, propane stove, water heater, and fireplace; a blacksmith shop with a 380-pound anvil and lots of antique tooling; an air-conditioned computer lab and dressing room with its own laundry chute; and an arm crane for loading a motorcycle aboard.

Florence has a Cummings turbo diesel engine that gets 12 to 16 miles per gallon. The chassis can accommodate up to 26,000 pounds, but Florence weighs in at a svelte 23,000 pounds. The couple has "sailed" more than 60,000 miles in Florence, exploring and performing all over the United States.

We BUY Horseshoes
$5
$10
GYPSY
TIME TRAVELERS
GYPSY
TIME TRAVELERS

We don't think John and Jeanine Carbett will give up site 24 in Malibu, California. Their 1957 Cardinal just looks too good backed up to a cliff overlooking the Pacific Ocean.

CHAPTER 5

How to Host a Rally

After a decade of attending and hosting rallies, we have experienced a variety of events— each one unique. Do not let the vast array of ideas and options prevent you from moving forward with hosting your own event. Start small and simple. It is more important that you move forward with a simple plan now than be intimidated by all the possible doings you may want to implement in the future. Being the host or wagon master can be rewarding. It also requires your time and the responsibility to make the arrangements and decisions that will arise before and during the event. Trailerites across the United States contact us to find out about rallies in their area. The ever-increasing interest in rescuing, restoring, and rallying in vintage RVs has created a demand for opportunities for folks to get together. We hope that you will take some of our ideas and host a rally in your region.

A 1947 Mercury woody and a vintage 1956 Airstream like "Ollie T," owned by Michael and Aedan Haworth of Sebastopol, California, are a setup that many people dream of. Photo by Hal Thoms Photography.

Headed into a quiet evening, the lights and décor create a mood that takes you back in time. Vintage canned ham trailers are so small that you can spread out. Some campgrounds will even let you double up in a site if your rally fills up.

Many campgrounds provide all of the amenities along with a level spot for your RV and a parklike setting. We suggest visiting the park to be sure it fits your needs before you plan an event there. Both photos on this page by Hal Thoms Photography.

A vintage trailer rally is nothing more than people with a common interest in preserving the nostalgia of the past getting together. You don't have to dream up a theme, hire a band, and commit to filling a hundred sites to host a rally. If there are no vintage rallies in your area, you can be the first to take on the role of wagon master. Use our experiences, and this book, to help you get started. It's as simple as one, two, three:

1. Pick a date.
2. Pick a location.
3. Let people know about the event.

Picking a date may be as simple as inviting others along on a trip you have already planned. Our first rally was based on a weekend that the park had prearranged activities. We literally just showed up and invited our friends to join us.

You will need to consider the weather in your region for the best turnout. We have attended rallies in the rain and during very cold weather at New Year's. We have had rallies that were vastly underattended due to heat. Your best bet is to choose a temperate, dry time of year that will appeal to most people. You may also want to make sure your date does not conflict with other vintage trailer rallies or major events in your immediate area. For a comprehensive list of trailer rallies in the United States, consult *Vintage Camper Trailers* magazine.

This color-coordinated setting features a neat little unidentified trailer. The large variety of brands made in the 1950s and '60s means we are always discovering new models and paint schemes. A rally is a great place to see and be seen!

Malibu Vintage Trailer Rally

Ahoy mates! Grab your pirate hats and join in the fun at the Malibu Vintage Trailer Rally. The annual pirate-themed rally is held at the Malibu Beach RV Park, with ocean-view sites located on a beautiful hillside overlooking the Pacific Ocean. The rally is open to all pre-1975 vintage trailers.

All photos on pages 158–63 by Kirsten Filonczuk.

These mates at the Malibu rally go
all out with costumes and games
around their pirate theme!

From left to right:
Erika Boyer, rally
host Alex Kleckner,
and Alex's mother,
Deon Kleckner.

A Boles Aero . . .

. . . a tiny trailer . . .

...and a Holiday House.

A vintage Airstream trailer.

A Shasta with its original patina.

This 2015 Shasta is a reissue of the original 1962 model.

Holidays can be a good time for a rally. Here are a few of our favorite holiday rally ideas:

New Year's: We get together with a small group of friends and barbecue prime rib. Everyone brings an upscale potluck side dish or dessert. We watch old movies or sit around the campfire until the New Year.

Valentine's Day: The host provides baked potatoes and the potluck is toppings for the potatoes or a valentine desert.

Cinco de Mayo: Trailerfiesta 2017 included a piñata contest, taco truck, and mariachi band. Elote (Mexican corn), churros, and quesadillas were served.

Saint Patrick's Day: Go green with an adult beverage and a vintage-inspired appetizer potluck. Think Jell-O molds, Spam, and Cheez Whiz. Present your appetizers on vintage serving dishes.

Halloween: Have your open house after dark with a chili cook-off contest and trick-or-treating. Instead of candy, trick-or-treat for a bite-sized dessert.

Trailerfiesta in Petaluma, California.

Señor Jake. Photo by Stan Drury.

Angelo Lacitinola and Faye Holland keep the griddle full of tasty quesadillas while wearing their sombreros.

Location, location, location. We like working with independently owned campgrounds and have had great interactions with chains like KOA and Jellystone. These large companies may have corporately held campgrounds or privately run franchises. We have worked with both to create several different types of rallies. The parks have worked closely with us and our group to grow Trailerfest to over 250 trailers. Most parks welcome vintage trailer rallies and offer some sort of group rates or free use of the park's amenities like group meeting areas, clubhouses, and cooking facilities. Contact the manager at your favorite park and let them know of your plans. Parks may be more receptive to working with you outside of their prime camping season. We often try to book dates right before, or right after, the campground's busy time. By doing that, we are a value to the property and receive the best pricing for our group.

A simple poster can be created to let the public know about your event.

Public campgrounds usually require online reservations, in advance, by each camper. Typically you are not able to work directly with these campgrounds or receive any group rates. I would encourage you to contact public parks and campgrounds individually to find out what their policies are. A public park can be a great space for a campout or boondocking, but may not be conducive to a larger rally. Other venues to consider are private residences with acreage, ranches, wineries, and fairgrounds. Anywhere with some open, outdoor area will work. If you select a location other than a campground, be sure to consider amenities like bathrooms, showers, and water and electrical hookups. Be very clear in your rally description about what will be provided and what will not be available. If generators are OK, set the hours of operation so everyone is clear and can plan for the weekend.

Letting people know about your rally has never been easier. The community is connected through a variety of clubs, social media websites, and the *Vintage Camper Trailers* magazine. Each one of these entities provides you with the ability to contact hobbyists interested in attending rallies across the United States. Your only investment is time in letting them know about your event so they can pass the information on to their members and subscribers.

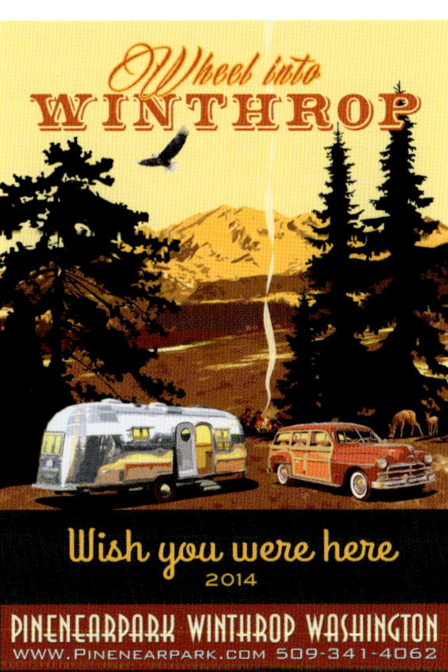

Pine Near RV Park in Winthrop, Washington, not only comes up with clever names, it also creates collector-quality posters for their events. Poster images provided by Pine Near RV Park.

RESERVATIONS

A vintage trailer rally is best if you can create a "vintage village" atmosphere. Whether you are hosting a dozen-trailer event or a hundred trailers, try to isolate a section of the park that you can fill. Having an area for the vintage trailer group makes the event more intimate and special than if you're scattered around the park. Try to avoid being hidden amongst the big white boxes with their pop outs and the diesel pushers that tower over your canned ham. Having fellow vintage trailerites for neighbors creates a fellowship among the midcentury aluminum enthusiasts. The beauty of positioning the vintage trailers in a group is particularly enchanting after dark. The glow of the amber shellac wood interior through the windows is enhanced by the brightly colored lights hanging along the vintage-styled awnings. Add to that a vintage record player crackling with one of yesterday's crooners or someone strumming a ukulele to take you back in time.

Reservations can be handled in one of two ways. A block of sites at the campground can be reserved by the host, to be held for a certain period of time in order for them to promote the rally. The host would collect the camping fees plus a rally fee and write one check to the park. Alternatively, each individual camper can make their reservation directly with the park. It is then up to the host to collect the rally fee to cover the incidental costs of the rally. Different rallies handle the reservations differently. Allowing the park to make the reservations directly with the individual campers increases the odds that nonvintage trailers will be scattered among the vintage group. Some parks are more able to help you handle the reservations to create a vintage village. Work with the park manager to determine what will be best for you, your event, and their reservation system.

Based on your agreement with the campground, you need to determine a must-register-by date and a cancellation policy. If a campground reserves space, they need a guarantee that those sites will be rented. Establish a date to release any unrented sites back to the campground without being charged. The cancellation policy will be based on the arrangements made with the park. When we host a rally, we have a no-refund policy unless the site is rented out to another camper. Because of the confusion that it creates and how busy we are in the time leading up to a rally, we do not offer refunds for cancellations made less than two weeks from the start of our rally. By that time we have paid most of the expenses and ordered all the food for the number of guests we are expecting.

RALLY FEES

Hosting rallies is not a get-rich quick scheme. Coming up with a rally fee to cover the costs that you will incur to host a rally is a critical part of organizing your event. Clearly your costs will vary greatly depending on the variety of activities that you plan. Obvious substantial costs would be food and entertainment. If you're only going to do a potluck, you may think that you have no costs. Consider if you will provide disposable plates and silverware for those that forget to bring some. Will you provide a substantial amount of a main dish to make sure everyone gets enough to eat? Will you provide any beverages? These things can add up when you are buying for a large group of people. Don't cut it so close that you end up having to pay out of pocket to cover all of the odds and ends.

Trailerfest has been an annual event for many years. We create a similar, but different, souvenir sticker for each year.

Photo by Hal Thoms Photography.

At Trailerfest we budget for a live band. This drives up our rally fee but we think it makes for a great event. The hard costs are offset by over 250 trailers, each contributing to the rally's expenses—not as easy to cover with a smaller group. There are many other ideas for inexpensive or free entertainment. At the first rally we hosted, we got together on a weekend that the park was already providing entertainment. It didn't cost us a thing. You may also have musicians, storytellers, or other types of entertainers right in your own circle of friends. Watching a vintage movie is another inexpensive event that people enjoy. Sometimes campgrounds can provide projectors and large screens if you don't have access to them otherwise. If you are going to hire a band, be clear on their electrical needs and who will provide the lighting and sound equipment. It is most common that the band provides their own sound equipment, but depending on the time of year and the time of performance you may need to provide some lighting.

Your rally fee also needs to cover small expenditures that can add up. Things like signs for the attendees to put in their windows that tell who they are, where they're from, and what kind of trailer they are in. You may want to produce a small souvenir like a sticker, magnet, or button to remind people of your event. There are many resources online to create these types of things in small quantities. They are certainly not necessary, but can be fun for those attending your rally to collect.

Depending on the size of your event or the requirements of the venue, you may want or need to purchase event insurance. Campgrounds, in our experience, do not require any insurance be purchased by the event host. Nontraditional camping facilities or event venues may require you to secure an insurance policy. We have found very affordable insurance options you can purchase for a specific event. A policy can be purchased online at a reasonable price and affords you a little peace of mind in the event an accident occurs. Please contact us if you need help locating event insurance for your rally.

At Trailerfest, we provide 8½ x 11 inch signs for the attendees so they can let others know a little bit about themselves. We have them printed on card stock because we order several hundred at a time, but you can make copies if your rally doesn't have many attendees or a big budget.

THEMES

You can create a theme for your rally. Trailerites can participate by decorating their trailers and dressing the part. A theme can be fun, however it's not a necessary element for a great rally. If this doesn't fit your style, just skip it. If it sounds like a good time, run with it and be as creative as you want to be. The options are endless. Pirates, 1960s hippies, 1970s disco, Mardi Gras, or whatever your favorite party theme may be. Here are some of our favorite themes:

Tiki: Start the weekend with a vintage appetizer potluck, complete with Hawaiian shirts and floral leis from the party store. A Hawaiian barbecue dinner with chicken, shrimp, macaroni salad, and white rice is always a winner.

Western: Have a Dutch oven and cast-iron cook-off. The contest also doubles as a potluck, with people encouraged to make chili, corn bread, or a dessert. Use repurposed trophies found at yard sales as kitschy prizes for the winners.

American Graffiti: There are all kinds of ways to spin the 1950s. Have a car show and a sock hop and break out your leather jackets and poodle skirts! Watch *The Long, Long, Trailer, American Graffiti,* or *Grease* on a big screen.

Christmas: We did "Christmas in the trailer park" in October at Trailerfest 2016 (see pages 170–75). The decorating possibilities were endless. People decorated their trailers with Christmas lights, Christmas trees, and vintage yard art decorations. Santa Claus showed up and we hired a train ride to take people around the park to see the more than 250 trailers on display. On Saturday night everybody chipped in to feed 600 people a Christmas ham dinner with all the fixings.

Mexican: Cinco de Mayo is a good time of year for a Mexican-themed rally. Obvious food choices and inexpensive sombreros for everyone will make your fiesta memorable.

Christmas in the Trailer Park

At Trailerfest, held at Yogi Bear's Jellystone Park, Lodi, California, in October 2016, we celebrated Christmas a couple months early—and fun was had by all!

The trailerite revelers enjoy some potluck.

Christmas dinner was served to more than 500 campers, including Mike and Sharon Kemp from Paradise, California, shown here.

Penny Cotter and Rachel Harp
serving Elvis Presley pancakes.

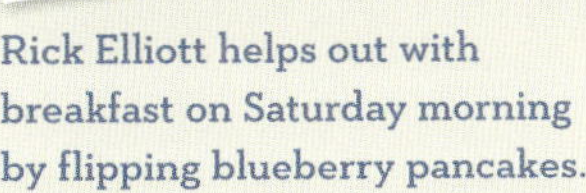

Rick Elliott helps out with
breakfast on Saturday morning
by flipping blueberry pancakes.

Christmas in the Trailer
Park was a theme that
everyone could relate to.
Decorating everything
from your trailer to your
seat at Christmas dinner
was easy.

Charles Diffey *is* Santa Claus. All photos on pages 172–73 by Glen Nichols.

Minibikes and vintage trailers are a natural mix.

From left to right: Glen Nichols, Mrs. Claus (Virginia Diffey), Debbie Nichols, and Santa Claus (Charles Diffey).

Glen and Debbie Nichols's trailer is all decorated for
Christmas in the Trailer Park.

The bike parade.

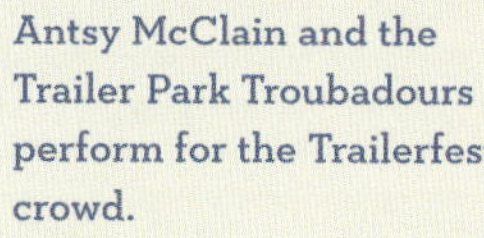

Antsy McClain and the Trailer Park Troubadours perform for the Trailerfest crowd.

We invited the Salvation Army because it wouldn't be Christmas without a bell ringer. We collected a truckload of toys, canned food, and some cash for the local charity.

Christmas dinner in the pavilion.

A picture frame made for fun photos. That's Randy and Charmaine Bonfantini (left), and Doug and Sue Owen (right).

A 1954 Kenskill eighteen-footer
owned by Joe and Cheryl Clarke of
Paradise, California, at the Woodson
Bridge Vintage Camper Rally (pages
176–77).

NAMING YOUR RALLY

*C*oming up with a clever name to differentiate your rally is a good way to set yourself apart in the growing calendar of vintage trailer events. Keep it simple. Try to come up with a name that is an identifier for the rally you are hosting or the area where it is located. This will give people who are seeking rallies to attend a quick idea of where or what your rally will be. Here are a handful of existing rallies:

Trailers in the Trees: Located among the redwoods in the Santa Cruz Mountains.

Rally at the River: Located on the Sacramento River at Woodson Bridge.

Rally at the Ranch: Boondocking on a 300-acre horse ranch.

Trailerfest: A large annual rally in Northern California.

Trailerfiesta: A Mexican-themed rally.

Halloween Vintage Trailer Mash: A Halloween rally (aka the Monster Mash).

Falluminum and **Alumapalooza:** Airstream rallies.

Ride the Wild Surf: A rally at the dunes in Newport Beach, California.

All-American Vintage Trailer Rally: Held on the Fourth of July weekend.

COMPETITION

The contests at a rally can begin before the rally even starts. The Tin Can Tourists are known to have a candelabra contest at many of their outings. Attendees are encouraged to be creative with their design of a centerpiece for their table at the potluck. In the tradition of the club, tin cans, ham cans, and even Spam cans are encouraged components of the sometimes elaborate creations. We have also had fun with piñata contests and chili cook-offs. We have learned over the years that for some, participating in these events is what they really enjoy. The great thing about a rally, with so many different people getting together, is that attendees may choose to participate in what they want. Not everyone will participate in everything and that's okay. Each time you host a rally you can repeat the popular activities or try new ones as you desire.

We have decided to keep contests and competitions based on things other than the trailers themselves. All too often we have seen hurt feelings, disappointment, and animosity infect a group of friends over something that doesn't really matter. The variety of trailers at a rally makes it nearly impossible to judge one against another. It becomes a contest of what you can afford. A true craftsman's work is apparent as soon as you step into some restored trailers. The finish detail and decorating that some owners achieve is obviously at a higher level than others. I enjoy touring these trailers and hearing about the builder's process as much as seeing the creative ways people on a tight budget have refurbished their trailers in order to participate in the vintage trailer hobby.

The trailer hobby appeals to such a vast variety of people, income levels, and abilities that a contest judging trailers can lead to more negative feelings than positive ones. We have seen judging at other rallies make for bad feelings that lead to gossip, and create division among people that have come together for the joy of vintage trailering.

If you would like to have a competition at your rally, we suggest judging things like best theme trailer decorating or best costume, or maybe even having a talent show. Our goal is to create events where everyone is welcome and does not feel they need to one-up everyone else.

Wes and Cindy Nordby's 1954 Aljoa at a vintage trailer rally at Bodega Bay, California.

OPEN HOUSE

Typically an open house runs from 10 a.m. until 2 or 3 p.m. on Saturday. Trailers are set up and staged for people to tour. Everybody breaks out their latest vintage finds and sets up their trailer and awning area with period-correct items from the era or theme they choose to identify with. An open house may be open to the public or just to the other campers at the park. Trailerites take great pride in their coaches. Some have found original specimens of America's past that were preserved for decades or stored out of the weather by the original owners. Others have painstakingly restored their trailers, investing both time and money. Most vintage trailers need some level of repair or restoration before their first rally. Decades of camping trips, kids, weather, and time have taken their toll over the years. An open house allows an opportunity to see what others have accomplished and share the owner's efforts with those who can appreciate their work.

The open house can be the highlight of a rally. Events where the public can come and appreciate the trailers are some of our favorites. We always tell people who are interested in purchasing a trailer and getting into the hobby to visit an open house first. Having the opportunity to experience the size and space of many different trailers at one time is helpful in their decision-making process. Once people attend a vintage trailer rally open house they're usually hooked on the hobby! Walking through the many trailers with their chenille bedspreads, Bakelite dinnerware, and shiny chrome percolators creates an atmosphere that takes many back to their childhoods. Tabletop fans, vintage radios and cameras, old thermoses, lanterns, and ice chests that we remember from our parents and grandparent's trailers take us back to what we perceive was a simpler time.

Many trailer owners will also display items that they have for sale. Picture a yard sale in front of a small house with wheels. They may have parts they've collected or period collectibles. Some crafty campers offer up everything from homemade jam to jewelry. Quilts, vintage-styled aprons, embroidered bags, and clothing are also likely to show up for sale. Vintage trailer restorers tend to be handy, clever, and resourceful people. Their creations usually have a vintage feel or trailer theme and are of amazing quality, using materials from silver and blown glass to old bottle caps. Most are doing it just for fun and charge modest prices.

An open house where people can buy and sell items, as shown here and on pages 180–81, is a typical activity at most rallies. Photos on pages 179–81 by Hal Thoms Photography, except for the left photo on page 181.

Don't miss the bargains and hand-crafted goodies that may be on display at an open house. You might find vintage camping gear and housewares to decorate your trailer or maybe locate a hard-to-find part. I have seen bonsai trees, jam, awning springs, silver jewelry, and hand-blown glass earrings shaped like trailers at a rally.

Vagabond Vintage

Vagabond Vintage is a pop-up store, with its show-room being Karen Fererro's 1964 Airstream. Part of Karen's Ozark Farm Girls business based in northwest Arkansas, it features jewelry made from recycled and repurposed old keys, vintage silverware, typewriter keys, old watches, grandma's buttons, and similar items most people would overlook or throw away. The style is a unique combination of country ranch girl romance and vagabond flair. Karen started out making spoon rings, and one inspiration led to another. Necklaces are a popular item and each one is unique and personal. Furniture, clothing, and home decor made from unexpected items are also displayed and sold in the trailer. Karen said, "I love collections and my art reflects that." Vagabond Vintage is a style, a feeling, and a way of life.

Photos by Tavi Ellis.

Photos by Karen Fererro (left and below).

Photo by Tavi Ellis.

At an open house that is not open to the public, we feel comfortable leaving our trailer open while we visit other people's vintage rigs. Vintage trailer enthusiasts typically have a respect and appreciation for the rarity and the fragile nature of other people's collectibles. We trust those who we camp with and are not concerned with our items walking away. With the public, on the other hand, you may have a different experience. It is not uncommon for larger rallies to attract hundreds of admirers and dreamers. Be aware that sometimes the public does not understand the hours and money involved in restoring the trailers, or the fact that they are old and often have parts and pieces that are not replaceable. They were not designed to have hundreds of people marching through, bouncing on the bed, or opening and closing every cupboard and closet door. They may think nothing of taking their kids, dogs, food, and beverages in with them. Depending on the condition of your trailer, you may want to set some limits with the public, who can unintentionally be tough on old trailers.

Consider the condition of your trailer and the impact hundreds of people walking through it will have. Your front step and support handle at your front door will receive a lot of use. You may want to use a sturdy modern step that sits on the ground, instead of the step that swings out from under your trailer. The swing-out steps on vintage trailers may not be sturdy enough to support the heavy traffic. If you *do* use the swing-out step, support it from underneath with a scissor jack or bottle jack from your tow vehicle. If your support handle is sturdy, no problem. If not, you can add a "please do not use" sign, or hide it with your sign that tells a little something about the trailer. Inside the trailer you may want to use ribbons or ropes to cordon off areas you don't want people to enter. Beds and dinette booths are typical areas that people will sit on. You can even use a vintage apron to span an area that you don't want people going past. Aprons are cute and period correct. Bathroom and refrigerator doors will get opened if you do not put some small "please look but don't touch" signs up. Our friends and fellow rally hosts Bob and Jacyn Gallagher have come up with a creative idea to combat nosy visitors: they position a mannequin head inside their refrigerator, where it does a good job startling the overly inquisitive tourist. I've seen others go so far as to use small motion-detector alarms to warn them when people are opening doors and cupboards they do not want them to.

Most of these types of events we really enjoy, and go back year after year. We have run into difficulties or challenges at festivals that are heavy drinking events or have a lot of small children. We sometimes use a tension curtain rod across the entrance door so people can look in and see the interior of the trailer but not enter it. This is a great option for a two-door trailer that allows the entire interior to be seen without going inside. If the event has more people than you can comfortably handle, limit the number of people inside your trailer at one time. This will help eliminate some issues. The public's admission price does not give them the right to search your trailer or disrespect your personal space. People that don't own vintage trailers are often not aware of the time or money the owners have invested in their coaches. It is fun to share the treasures that we have found, preserved, or restored, but we must also protect them from unnecessary wear and tear.

This will surely startle nosy visitors who want to open every cupboard and your fridge.

Casual camping at the Bothe-Napa Valley State Park show.

Guest speakers: Have an industry expert, respected restorer, or camping product vendor give a class on their area of expertise or a how-to on their product. We have done presentations ourselves on how to best buy and sell trailers and how to host a rally.

Miniature golf: Designated trailers are selected to form a miniature golf course. Campers, dressed in period garb, go from trailer to trailer to see if they can make par. If you like you can add a libation at each hole you make.

Scavenger hunt: An old-school-type scavenger hunt for camping-related items can be fun, especially for the kids.

Talent show: Get as fancy as you want, with an entertaining moderator to introduce each of the predetermined acts, or an informal "come as you are and show us what you've got!" Many parks have an area with a stage, gazebo, or similar area that can be used for your show.

Crafts: Many people enjoy crafting and teaching others to craft. Find someone in the group who enjoys teaching others their craft. (You probably already know who this is.) Handmade items like penny rugs, knitting, quilts, and jewelry can all take on a vintage trailer spin for the rally. Cooking classes on homemade ice cream, jam, and campfire recipes are also winners.

A pajama, bike, or pet parade gets everybody up and moving around the park early Saturday morning. Photo by Hal Thoms Photography.

The Malibu Vintage Trailer Rally is a pirate-themed rally, with pirate-themed activities. Photo by Kirsten Filonczuk.

GROUP FOOD IDEAS

Pancake breakfast: You can do this on the cheap and have fun with it too. We have done Elvis Presley pancakes with peanut butter, banana, and bacon. Sprinkle precooked bacon pieces into the pancake batter on the griddle before you flip them. You can add blueberries to pancakes before you flip them too. By adding the berries to the individual cakes on the griddle, you will not turn your entire batch of batter blue-gray. Another fruit topping is strawberries—best when they are in season—with whipped cream. We have done pancakes with chocolate chips, cinnamon sugar, and tres leches sauce at our Mexican-themed rally. You can get creative with pancakes and offer a fun morning get-together for just a little effort and expense. If your budget permits you can elevate a simple pancake breakfast with sausage links. We use the precooked ones that are easy to warm up and brown in a huge cast-iron skillet.

Other breakfast ideas: Oatmeal can be made in Crock-Pots or a large rice cooker. Toppings can range from fresh fruit to brown sugar and nuts. Yogurt is a good addition to this healthy breakfast menu because you can utilize the same toppings.

Donuts are easy and not very expensive. Preorder from the closest shop with great donuts and they will be ready to pick up early in the morning.

Waffles made on vintage waffle irons add that vintage touch to your rally. Invite everyone to bring their favorite midcentury waffle iron or their favorite waffle topping. Make sure you have plenty of extension cords and power to run several irons at one time.

Get toasted. Like the waffle irons, many trailerites have vintage toasters. A good Sunday morning farewell breakfast can include homemade breads, butters, jams, or jellies.

Food is always a good reason for everyone to get together.

Vintage waffle irons loaded with batter make for a fun breakfast for a small- to medium-sized rally.

Pie irons are another fun twist to an interactive breakfast. Everybody brings their own iron and some bread or filling. Our family's favorite is what we call a Grandma Mandy. My grandmother would fill a pie iron with two pieces of buttered white bread with jelly and American cheese.

A Dutch oven biscuits-and-gravy feast is a back-to-basics way for everyone to have a hearty breakfast. Divide up the work with some campers making biscuits or cobblers and other campers responsible for the sausage gravy.

Root beer floats: An easy and economical cool treat for a warm afternoon or evening. Who doesn't like root beer floats?

S'mores or wadinger buffet: You can go crazy with this one. Go safe or let your imagination run wild with toppings and fillings for these two campfire favorites. The more common s'more is typically two pieces of graham cracker with a chocolate bar and a toasted marshmallow sandwiched in the middle. A wadinger is made by wrapping a refrigerator biscuit around a wooden dowel or a stick (coat it with mineral oil first) and baking it over a campfire. Once cooked, you slide your biscuit off the dowel and fill it with sweet or savory goodies. Anything from pudding and fresh fruit to scrambled eggs and sausage. I have even seen spaghetti used as a filling!

S'mores for everyone! Avoid the smoke and let everyone toast their marshmallows by using Sterno in these wooden troughs filled with decorative rocks.

Homemade ice cream: We are fortunate to have an in-house ice cream maker. Martha K. never disappoints with her homemade ice cream she makes with vintage ice cream makers for everyone at the campground. Maple bacon is a crowd-pleaser, but you can involve everyone who wants to make their favorite flavor. Have a get-together after the open house for a cool afternoon treat or as an after-dinner dessert competition.

AFTER DARK

Evenings in the trailer park evoke their own magic. Strolling through the park after dark you will be captivated by the amber glow of soft lights through the windows of the carefully restored RVs. Awnings may be adorned with string lights and you'll likely find groups of friends around campfires catching up and telling stories. Impromptu jam sessions on guitars, ukuleles, and an occasional washboard is not unusual. If you're spotted lurking in the shadows you will likely be invited to join the campfire and tell your tales. Before everyone turns in for the night you're likely to hear distant conversations and laughter mixed with the sounds that the night creatures and Mother Nature add to the mystique of the darkness.

THE LAST DAY (HIT THE TRAIL, JACK)

As quickly as the campsites filled up just a few days before, by noon on Sunday the once jam-packed park is empty again. Checkout time is usually around 11:00 a.m. By Sunday campers are spent. Some have long trips home, and safe towing speeds can take a little longer to get where you're going. Sunday mornings we make a big pot of coffee so people can grab a cup as they say goodbye and head out. Don't make big plans for Sunday morning, as most people are just packing and getting on the road. One thing we have learned over the years is to take down our awning the night before we leave. The night air, or worse yet an unexpected sprinkle, will cause you to have a damp piece of canvas to wrestle into a storage bag or compact area. If this happens, make sure to unfold the awning as soon as you can to let it dry out. Dampness will lead to mold and rot.

We usually get on the road and meet up with a few folks at the nearest breakfast joint for one last goodbye before we head home. It's about this time I start thinking about what we'll do at our next event! I like to reflect on things that worked and things that didn't. At our Trailerfest rally each year we never have the same theme or activities. I think it keeps it fun and new so every year we aren't just going through the motions. So far it seems to be working. Trailerfest is sold out a year in advance, with over 250 trailers, and we all seem to have a good time.

We always take down our awning the night before we leave. If you wait until the morning, the canvas may be damp with dew. You don't want to fold it up with any moisture or it can get moldy and smell or become discolored.

SUMMARY

If you haven't figured it out yet, a rally is just a good excuse to get together with friends, socialize, be silly, and eat. We have laid out most of what we have learned hosting and attending rallies with anywhere from 10 to 300 trailers in attendance. We didn't start big, and it is still our opinion that bigger is not always better. We look forward to the times when it's just six to eight couples, a campfire, and a great meal that everybody chipped in for.

Our motivation for writing this book was to encourage you to host a rally in your area. We hope we've provided you with some guidance, but did not scare you into thinking you had to arrange a huge event. I can't stress enough that it is best to keep it simple and start small. If your rally grows into a larger event over several seasons, there are people that will help you. If you need another push, you can always call us.

Glossary

Barn find—A trailer found in storage after many years. Usually in good or better-than-average shape as a result of being protected from the elements.

Boondocking—Camping with your trailer in a location (often out in the "boondocks") that doesn't have water, sewer, or electrical hookups—and is usually free. Also known as "dry camping."

Bread loaf—A trailer often thought to look like a horse trailer in the front, with a slightly sloping rear area (usually over sixteen feet long).

Canned ham—A small trailer (usually under sixteen feet) that has a profile shape of a canned ham.

Caravan—A group of trailers traveling to a destination together. Also the term for "trailer" in Great Britain.

Field find—A trailer found stored outdoors after many years.

Glamper—A combination of the words "glamour" and "camper," this refers to a trailer (or the trailerite that owns it), typically decorated with a decidedly feminine touch, including frills, doilies, linens, and happy colors.

Glamping—Glamorous camping.

Host—The person who organizes a rally.

No-host—An unhosted event, like a potluck meal; bring your own beverages, silverware, plates, and napkins.

Open house—A designated time that trailers are decorated and staged for visitors. It can be for the public to attend or just for the other campers at a rally.

Pie iron—A long-handled, clam-shell-style compartment you line with bread, fill with preserves, cheese, meat, or whatever you want, close the lid, and toast over the fire.

Potluck—A meal where everyone brings a dish and shares.

Rebuilt—A trailer that's been extensively torn down and put back together with new materials and components.

Refurbished—A trailer repaired to a useable condition, but not to the more extensive level of "restored."

Restored—A trailer repaired to like-new or better-than-original condition.

S'mores—Toasted marshmallows and chocolate bars melted between two graham crackers.

SOTF—Sisters on the Fly.

TCT—Tin Can Tourists.

Teardrop—A small trailer that's shaped like a teardrop, sleeps two, and is so compact you can't stand up inside.

Trailerite—An individual in the trailer hobby.

VCT—*Vintage Camper Trailers* magazine.

Vintage vendor—Someone that sells goods from a vintage trailer.

Wadinger—A biscuit dough cooked over a campfire on a wooden dowel and then filled with either sweet or savory goodies (also spelled "whadinger").

Wagon master—Another term for "host."

YOM—Year of manufacture (referring to when a trailer was built).

CLOSED